Getting Started with
Mortared Stonework

Getting Started with
Mortared Stonework

WALLS, PATIOS, FIREPLACES, COLUMNS & MORE

Cody Macfie

LARK BOOKS

A Division of Sterling Publishing Co., Inc.
New York

EDITORS: Paige Gilchrist, Terry Krautwurst, and Kathy Sheldon

ART DIRECTOR: Thom Gaines

COVER DESIGNER: Barbara Zaretsky

PRINCIPAL AND COVER PHOTOGRAPHERS:
Stewart O'Shields and Sean A. Trapp

ILLUSTRATOR: Don Osby

ASSISTANT EDITOR: Rebecca Guthrie

ASSOCIATE ART DIRECTOR: Shannon Yokeley

ART PRODUCTION ASSISTANT: Jeff Hamilton

EDITORIAL ASSISTANCE: Delores Gosnell

EDITORIAL INTERN: Megan S. McCarter

ART INTERN: Ardyce E. Alspach

DEDICATION

This book is dedicated to John Macfie, my father, and Jim Macfie, my uncle, for gracefully laying the foundation upon which my knowledge of this subject matter was built. They raise my standards and make it seem effortless.

Library of Congress Cataloging-in-Publication Data

Macfie, Cody, 1976-
  Getting started with mortared stonework : walls, patios, fireplaces, columns & more / Cody Macfie.— 1st ed.
    p. cm.
  Includes index.
  ISBN 1-57990-665-6 (hardcover)
    1. Stonemasonry. I. Title.
TH5401.M33 2006
693'.1—dc22
  2005024690

10 9 8 7 6 5 4 3 2 1

First Edition

Published by Lark Books, A Division of
Sterling Publishing Co., Inc.
387 Park Avenue South, New York, N.Y. 10016

Text © 2006, Cody Macfie
Photography © 2006, Lark Books unless otherwise specified
Illustrations © 2006, Lark Books

Distributed in Canada by Sterling Publishing,
c/o Canadian Manda Group, 165 Dufferin Street
Toronto, Ontario, Canada M6K 3H6

Distributed in the United Kingdom by GMC Distribution Services,
Castle Place, 166 High Street, Lewes, East Sussex, England BN7 1XU

Distributed in Australia by Capricorn Link (Australia) Pty Ltd.,
P.O. Box 704, Windsor, NSW 2756 Australia

If you have questions or comments about this book, please contact:
Lark Books
67 Broadway
Asheville, NC 28801
(828) 253-0467

Manufactured in China

For information about custom editions, special sales, premium and corporate purchases, please contact Sterling Special Sales Department at 800-805-5489 or specialsales@sterlingpub.com.

Contents

Introduction

The inspiration for this book came to me last year as a group of stonemasons and I were working on top of eight sets of scaffolding, 56 feet above the ground. My uncle and my father (both master stonemasons) and I were only a few stones away from finishing a tall chimney. We were feeling optimistic—perhaps less because we were near completion and more because the end of a hard day of labor was near.

I watched my uncle look for a stone to set on his corner. The one he chose had potential, but I could see right away it wasn't perfect. He grabbed his blunt chisel and four-pound hammer and went to work. After perfecting the side that would sit upright on the corner, he made a seat for the rock, and then proceeded to flatten the top so it could make a seat for the next one. Minutes later he had an indefectible corner. It was solid and it looked as if fate had placed the perfect rock.

I asked him if he considered himself an artist and he modestly replied, "No, it's probably nothing more than on-the-job training." I thought about it for a while and decided later that he was only half right. On-the-job training might have increased the efficiency by which he sculpted that rock, but the outcome was nothing less than artistry.

It's virtually impossible to build a chimney as we did that day without some degree of experience and a few extra hands, but smaller projects can be managed on your own, and the tangible sense of accomplishment you'll feel at the end of the day is unequaled. Perhaps you've done a bit of dry-laid stonework but the thought of attempting mortared stonework intimidates you. Don't let it! With the proper tools and the right materials, along with a little time and heavy lifting, anyone can create a variety of stone projects (and a wider variety than you can build with dry-laid stone). Laying a flagstone patio, veneering a fireplace, or building a wall can all be accomplished without a large crew. In fact, once you get started, you'll realize that you need only a bit of practice and patience to become skilled in the craft of mortared stonework.

I've written this book to help you with that endeavor. In the first four chapters we'll take an up-close look at stones, mortar, and the tools and equipment you'll be using. In the following chapter, I'll discuss patterns and styles for mortared stonework, and then I'll cover all the basics. The rest of the book presents a wide range of projects you can build with mortared stone. These vary from constructing a simple bench to covering a ho-hum brick fireplace with stone.

I assure you that when you've completed that first project, you'll discover it was easier than you thought and more satisfying than you might have imagined. You may not become a master stonemason immediately, but just as the perfect corner was waiting inside that rock for my uncle's chisel and hammer, I'm betting there's a stone artist waiting inside you.

What Is Mortared Stonework?

Make no mistake—I love all types of stonework including the dry-laid, nonmortared type that you might think of first when you envision a rustic stone wall bordering a farm field or country road. In fact, I would no more pass up an opportunity to build a dry-stacked wall than I would a mortared one. Regardless of whether mortar is involved, stonework is stonework—the same good heft of rock, the same shaping and fitting techniques, the same hard but satisfying labor.

But in many cases it's important, or outright necessary, to stick your stonework together with mortar to give it strength and permanence. And that, in essence, is what mortared stonework is all about. Stone can't support itself when it gets to a certain point. For instance, you don't absolutely need mortar if you're building a small retaining wall that will be used mainly to change the level of the landscape. However, if it's more than a few feet tall and it's going to retain soil and roots, mortar is critical.

Mortared, rather than dry-laid, stonework is required for building tall freestanding walls and retaining walls, for covering wood-sheathed walls or concrete-block chimneys, for using flagstone or slate on a concrete base for a patio or walkway, and for building sturdy columns.

Also, mortar makes it possible to build with the most irregular and unusually shaped stones that exist in nature. This doesn't mean that mortar eliminates the need for carefully trimming and stacking stones, or that it makes those jobs any easier. But it does mean that mortar opens more options to you, in terms of the types and shapes of stone you can use. Smooth, water-rounded river rocks, for example, would be less than ideal for a nonmortared stacked-stone structure, but if you set those rocks in a unifying bed of mortar, they can be used to create strong, attractive stonework that will stand the test of time.

On the other hand, practicality and function are hardly the only reasons for using mortar in stonework. In addition to strength and permanence, mortared stonework can be created in a tremendous variety of distinctive styles and patterns, making it uniquely flexible and adaptable to all sorts of situations. Whether your home is modern or rustic, urban or rural, you can build mortared stonework that reflects and complements its surroundings.

Mortar allows you to build sturdy, long-lasting features (top) and to use round rocks, such as river stones (lower right), in projects.

Dry-stack style

Jointed style

Styles of Mortared Stonework

There are two basic styles of mortared stonework: dry-stack and jointed. *Dry-stack* style, as you might guess, mimics traditional nonmortared dry-stack stonework. Mortar is used, but it's placed mostly behind the stones, bonding them to a wood-sheathed or concrete-block structure, or to the backfill in a retaining wall or planter. Stones are shaped and stacked as tightly together as possible. Small amounts of mortar are spread between courses of stones, too, to tie the stones together, but any visible mortar is scratched away before it dries, leaving the remaining mortar in the shadowed recesses, out of view.

Jointed mortared stonework, on the other hand, leaves visible mortar around the stones. The lines of mortar, which may be flush with the stones' surface or raised or indented, are visual elements—their effect is usually subtle, but always significant. Picture a little stone cottage in the countryside, or an imposing Medieval castle, and your mental image will likely be of jointed stonework. A flagstone patio is another example of jointed work.

Structurally, both styles of using mortar in stonework serve the same purpose: to glue the elements together. Aesthetically, however, each style offers distinctly different looks and options. We'll discuss this in more detail in the chapter called Pattern & Style. It's a good idea to become familiar with the steps involved in both styles—not just their looks—before deciding which to use in a given project. Some kinds of stone are more appropriate for one style or the other, and each style's techniques offer advantages and disadvantages. Dry-stack style, for instance, may require more work with a hammer and chisel to get the stones to fit tightly. The jointed style adds some steps and requires you to pay careful attention while making the mortar.

Veneer

Types of Mortared Stonework

Solid-stone construction

It's also important to understand the distinctions between two basic types, or techniques, of mortared stonework: solid stone and veneer.

In the old days, all mortared stonework was *solid stone:* the structures were self-supporting. Building foundations were built 12 to 16 inches thick, with stone exposed on both sides and, usually, stone backfill in the middle, all held together by mortar. Chimney cores were not made of studs and wood sheathing or block. The stonemason built the entire chimney structure out of stone. Solid-stone construction is seldom used anymore except for stone walls and columns. It requires so much stone that it can be very expensive.

These days, most mortared stonework that you see is *veneer,* a layer of stone covering an understructure of some sort, usually wood sheathing, concrete block, or a concrete pad. Foundation walls are built of concrete or block and are then covered with stone. Specialists use wood, metal, and other modern materials to install the working parts of a new fireplace—the firebox, dampers, flue liner, and chimney—before the stonemason comes in to veneer with stone.

There are two types of veneer: *thick veneer,* which is 5 to 8 inches or more in thickness, and *thin veneer,* which is 1 to 4 inches thick.

Thick veneer consists of stones stacked on top of one another in courses, each supported by the stones beneath. The space between the back of the stones and the surface of the structure is filled with small stones and mortar, gluing the veneer in place.

Thin veneer consists of thin stones (less than 2 inches) that are literally stuck to the surface—say, a concrete block column or foundation wall. That explains the other term for this kind of veneer: *stick-on.* The stones are supported by an especially sticky type of mortar applied to the back of each stone. Thin veneers are generally only as thick as the stones themselves plus a ¼-inch layer of mortar holding them to the surface—for a total thickness of about 1 to 2 inches.

Regardless of the style or techniques you might choose for a given project, remember that mortared stonework is no more difficult than dry-laid stonework. True, there are additional steps in making the right mortar and applying it to hold everything together, and sometimes you'll also need to pour a concrete footing or pad to provide a project with a stable foundation. But those tasks are mere matters of a little time, not special skill or effort, and that small investment of a couple of extra hours you put into mortaring your stonework pays a dividend in years: stonework that stands strong and permanent.

Thick veneer

Thin veneer

Whenever I'm working with stone, I think of the old stonemasons who migrated here to the mountains of western North Carolina many years ago. What tools and techniques did they use to manipulate the face of a stone? How did they keep a flagstone floor level while setting each stone across an uneven mortar bed? The answers are simple. They did it the same way I do it today and the same way you will build your own projects.

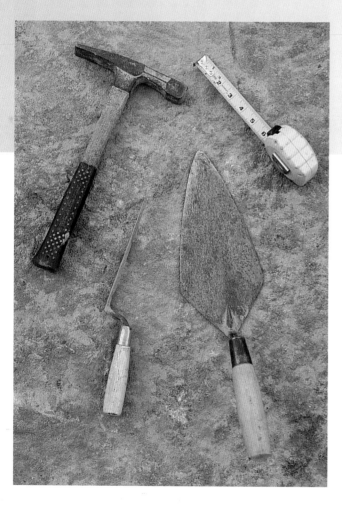

They used the sharp edge of a brick hammer and a stonemason's hammer with a blunt chisel to shape each stone. They used trowels to place mortar between stones. They used strings and levels to make sure their work was plumb and even.

Stonemasons' tools are simple, user-friendly, easy to find, and (usually) inexpensive. You can buy most of the tools you'll need for the projects in this book at your local hardware store or home improvement center, or at yard and estate sales. The techniques you'll learn here for using the tools are designed to help you complete your project safely and efficiently.

Basic Tool List

Here are the basic tools you'll need for most mortared stone projects. Sometimes you'll need more tools and sometimes fewer, depending on the exact project. If several people are going to be helping you on a project, you may need more than one of certain tools such as wheelbarrows and shovels.

- Stonemason's hammer, 3 to 4 pounds
- Brick hammers, 14 to 24 ounces
- Blunt and sharp chisels
- Rubber mallet
- Wheelbarrow
- Mortar hoe
- Brick mason's trowel
- Tuck pointer
- Square point shovel
- Whiskbroom
- Mattock
- Pry bar
- Tape measure
- Level
- Line level
- Plumb bob and string
- Safety essentials (page 23)

Tools for Breaking & Shaping Stone

Learning to break and shape stones requires patience and practice. Your first attempts are bound to be less than stellar and to result in some wasted stone. That's okay—getting the hang of shaping stone is the kind of thing that comes gradually. With a little practice, hitting the stone just the right way in just the right spot will become second nature to you. In the meantime, having the proper tools on hand will make the learning process much easier. A good selection of hammers, chisels, and saws will get you started on the right track.

Hammers

There are many hammers that will effectively cut and break stone. However, you won't need all of them all the time. For general use, I prefer a 24-ounce brick hammer, a 4-pound rock hammer, and—when I need to break larger stones—a 12-pound sledgehammer.

Left to right: brick chisel, sharp chisel, blunt chisel

Brick hammer and rock hammer

Rubber mallets

Brick hammers are usually sold in 14- to 24-ounce sizes, with both fiberglass and wooden handles. They're used for trimming the faces of smaller stones or the edges of flagstones. I prefer the heavier 24-ounce hammer with a fiberglass handle. I've found that it'll last longer and deliver a more solid hit to the stone than a wooden-handle hammer.

Rock hammers, also called stonemason's hammers or spalling hammers, are available in 3- and 4-pound weights. The head is blunt on one end and sharply wedge-shaped on the other. I like the 4-pound size and use the blunt end for making smaller stones of large ones and for striking chisels. The sharp edge is great for splitting stone.

Sledgehammers are usually sold in 8- to 12-pound sizes. Though I've used a 20-pound sledgehammer, I don't recommend it. You can end up too exhausted to pick up the pieces of the stone after you break it. Use a 12-pound hammer for breaking up large pieces of hard, dense stone such as granite, and a lighter hammer for less dense stone, such as sandstone or limestone.

A **mallet** is indispensable for setting flat stones such as pavers, flagstones, capstones, and hearthstones firmly in a mortar bed. I prefer a mallet with a rubber head, though you can purchase them with plastic, leather, or wooden heads.

Chisels

Chisels are used for scoring, shaping, and refining the edges of stones. Although a rock hammer is sufficient in most situations, using a chisel allows you to strike the stone more precisely and accurately, and produces a better cut with a cleaner edge.

The most inexpensive and easiest-to-find chisels that can be used for masonry work are **cold chisels**, which are made of tempered steel and have a two-sided beveled blade ranging from 1 to 2 inches wide. **Brick chisels** are similar but have a wider blade. Both types can usually be found at hardware stores. Keep in mind, however, that these chisels won't stand up to prolonged use on stone.

Most stonemasons use heavier chisels made of alloy steel with carbide tips. They're much more expensive than regular tempered-steel chisels but they hold an edge much longer. The two basic chisels in this category are the **sharp chisel**, which is also called a hand-tracer chisel and the **blunt chisel**. The blunt chisel (or hand-set chisel) is used primarily for making corners or straight faces and for removing large knots or high spots on a stone, while the sharp chisel is used for scoring and splitting stones. This is my favorite chisel since I find it to be the most versatile. A hand-point chisel is used to chisel away small knots.

Cold chisels, brick chisels, and **hand-point chisels** are widely available at hardware stores and home improvement centers. Carbide-tipped chisels, on the other hand, are usually available only through specialty masonry tool suppliers; check your local phone directory and the Internet for sources.

Electric angle grinder and chop saw

Hand-point chisels

Saws

An **electric angle grinder** or **circular saw** equipped with a 4- to 7-inch diamond stone-cutting blade is useful for scoring thin veneer stone and for cutting manufactured stone. I also use a **small angle grinder** with a grinding wheel to cut metal lath, which I install on vertical surfaces prior to thin-veneer stonework (see page 76).

A **chop saw** or **masonry cut-off saw** with a 12- to 14-inch-diameter diamond blade or grinding wheel can be used to score thick stones, cut flagstone or thin veneer stones, and create mantel supports and lintels. These saws can be found at your local hardware store or equipment rental center. Make sure you follow all directions when operating these tools. They're powerful, expensive, and physically taxing to use. Make sure, too, that your project is appropriate for stone cut with a power saw, which has a cleaner, less rustic look than hammered or chiseled stone.

One final and important note: Always wear safety glasses when cutting and breaking stone and a dust mask when using any masonry saw.

Brick mason's trowel

Pointing trowel

Tuck pointer

Stucco trowel

Tools for Mortaring

Trowels

Trowels are the essential tools for spreading and otherwise working with mortar. They come in a variety of types, sizes, and shapes. Choosing the right one to use is mostly a matter of matching the trowel to the amount of mortar you need to apply and the size of the area in which you need to place it.

A **brick mason's trowel** is for picking up and spreading mortar on a surface before placing the next layer, or course, of stone. It's also the tool of choice for filling and packing mortar in the space behind the stone on vertical veneering projects such as a concrete block wall. They're available with blades ranging from about 5 to 6 inches wide at the "heel" and 10 to 13 inches long. I like a medium size for general mortaring work.

A **pointing trowel** is for working mortar into small spaces. The blade of a pointing trowel is shaped much like a brick mason's trowel but is more pointed at the end and smaller overall. Pointing trowel blades range from 4 to 7 inches long and 2 to 3 inches wide. Pointing trowels can also be used for raking the joints of both horizontal and vertical stonework.

A **tuck pointer**, or scratching tool, is for packing mortar into small, hard-to-reach spaces and for scratching out or raking joints—removing the front portion of fresh mortar from joints so that the remaining mortar is recessed and less visible. Tuck pointer blades are long, straight, and appropriately narrow, ranging from $\frac{1}{4}$ to 1 inch wide.

A **stucco trowel** has a flat, rectangular metal blade with a handle mounted directly over it. The tool is used for applying a scratch coat, or thin layer of mortar, over metal lath to prepare a surface for applying thin veneer (see page 76).

A **whiskbroom** is the best tool for sweeping away the excess mortar left after scratching out joints. It can also be used to clean a small masonry surface area, such as a dirty concrete footing or block wall, before spreading mortar.

Tools for Moving Stone and Materials

No matter what project you're pursuing, you'll need an efficient way to move your stone, mortar, and other materials around the site.

Wheelbarrows

A sturdy **metal wheelbarrow** is a good investment for any stone project. Wheelbarrows are sold with buckets ranging from 4 to 6 cubic feet. I prefer the larger size. In any case, be careful not to overload it or you'll have a hard time moving it around—and even a good wheelbarrow will quickly wear out under too much weight. I usually load my wheelbarrow no more than half full of stones, and mix no more than one batch of mortar in it at a time. Position materials in the center of the wheelbarrow's bucket for easy maneuvering. Avoid purchasing wheelbarrows with two wheels. Stonework creates many obstacles on a site—tools, bits of rock, piles of sand, and other materials—making it hard to maneuver a two-wheeler around.

A strong board makes a good ramp for pushing a wheelbarrow up into a house or onto a porch. You'll need a second person to help you move a load of stones up a hill—one person pushes the wheelbarrow from the back while the other helps steady the load and pulls from the front.

Buckets

Five-gallon buckets come in handy for all sorts of jobs. I use them to transfer stone to scaffolding, to hold mortar on scaffolding, to pour water into the mix when I'm making mortar, to hold tools, to hold soupy mortar, and on and on. Make sure the bucket is clean before adding sand or mortar to it. The best way to clean a bucket is to lightly tap the outside of it with a hammer to loosen any dry mortar on the sides. Then rinse the container thoroughly with water.

Other Necessary Tools

You'll need a variety of other tools, too, for almost any mortared stonework project.

Shovels are a must for loading sand into a mixer or wheelbarrow, digging footings, scraping off the top of a poured footing, and general job site cleanup. A square point shovel has a square blade and a round point has a round blade. I prefer to use a square point most of the time, but a round point makes digging a footing easier.

A **mattock** is the tool of choice for loosening dense dirt and embedded rocks from the ground and for digging small footings. Use a **pry bar** to pry large stones out of the ground or to move stones in a rock pile.

Framing squares are used to mark a corner before you start the stonework.

You'll need a **tape measure** for just about everything related to stonework: to measure stones, to help you maintain a consistent depth between the face of a stone and the wall when veneering with stone, and to measure the size of a footing, just to name a few uses.

You'll need a **level** to keep horizontal surfaces flat and properly pitched, and to plumb vertical surfaces, and to mark straight lines on stones before cutting

them with a hammer. Levels are sold in 2- to 6-foot lengths; typically you'll need to check a variety of spans on a given job, so having both a short level and a long one is convenient, though not absolutely necessary. Two-foot levels are good for leveling horizontal stones on veneers. Six-foot levels are convenient for laying stones on large patios and sidewalks, and a four-footer is a great general-purpose level for anything.

A **plumb bob** is a weight at the end of a line used to mark points from which a string can be tied as a guide line for making straight corners on wall ends or column corners. A **line level** hooks over a string pulled horizontally between two points; move the string's ends up or down as needed to center the bubble and level the string, then use the line as a height guide for a wall or other project.

Use **scaffolding** and **walk boards** whenever you're working on a project that's more than shoulder-high. A ladder will not provide the support and stability you need while working with heavy stone. Walk boards can be lightweight aluminum clip-on types or pieces of 2x8, or wider, treated lumber.

Heavy Equipment

The only heavy equipment you might need for a stonework project is a **front-end loader**, a **track hoe**, or a **dump truck**. A front-end loader is a wheeled vehicle with a hydraulic scoop for excavating and loading loose material. It's useful for moving large amounts of stone around a large job site. A track hoe makes short work of digging long and/or deep footings. A dump truck can ease the frustration of waiting for your local stone supplier to bring you more stone when you run out. If you need heavy equipment, check with local heavy-equipment rental companies or ask a grading contractor or construction firm to see if they can do the work for you.

Safety Essentials

Always wear **safety glasses**, **heavy-duty gloves**, and **steel-toed boots** when working with stone. If you're working on a construction site or on scaffolding, wear a **hard hat**. In addition, if you'll be mixing mortar for an extended period of time or in a place where the cement dust won't dissipate quickly, wear an appropriate **dust mask**. Fresh concrete is caustic. Wear **rubber boots**, **protective clothing**, **gloves**, and **eye protection** when working with concrete. Common sense is the best way to prevent accidents from happening on a job. Using the right safety equipment is a good start.

A Guide to Stone

One of the most exciting parts of stonework is the process of finding and choosing stone. For some masons, this involves tearing down an old rock chimney in the woods, or searching a creek bed for flat stones. For others, it can mean simply spending some time at a local stone supply yard.

The type of stone you choose affects not only the end result's overall look—its pattern, texture, color, and more—but also the complexity of the job, the tools and equipment you'll need, and the techniques you'll apply. Some types of stone split easily and some do not, some break uniformly and some randomly, some are porous and some are slick. Some kinds of stone have a formal appearance while others impart a rustic look; some evoke images of ancient Druid monuments or New England farm fences, while others are perfect for contemporary structures.

All of these factors and more come into consideration as you take the steps of finding the right stone. As you sort through the possibilities, considering some and eliminating others, the stone itself will help you define and visualize how you want your project to look.

From beginning to end, it's all about the stone. The more you learn about it, the more its varied possibilities will open to you, and the more stone projects you'll want to pursue.

Types of Stone

You don't have to be a geologist to create great mortared stonework, but it helps to have a basic understanding of how the various kinds of stone you'll encounter at a stone yard look and behave.

There are three broad geologic classes of rock. Each has properties that are significant to a stonemason.

Igneous rock was formed under conditions of intense heat or by the solidification of volcanic magma on or below the earth's surface. As a result, this rock, which includes granite and basalt, is extremely dense and hard and is therefore more difficult than other kinds to split, break, or trim.

Igneous rock

On the other hand, some kinds of igneous rock look particularly good and are a bargain to boot. Granite is the most widely used type of igneous rock for stonework. Most stone yards have bulk piles of granite, which can be great for hand-picking rock for retaining or freestanding walls. Sometimes granite is so inexpensive that you can use it economically for backfill in retaining walls.

Sedimentary rock, such as limestone and sandstone, is the easiest type to split, trim, and otherwise work with. This stone was formed from material that was deposited as sediment by water, wind, or ice and then

Sedimentary rock

consolidated over thousands of years by pressure. It's usually available at stone yards, but because of its workability and popularity, it's also usually more expensive. Sandstone and limestone are good choices for most projects. They're much easier to manipulate and trim than granite.

Metamorphic rock, you may recall your science teacher telling you, includes any rock that has been changed into another kind of rock by chemical action or by pressure or heat. Marble, for instance, is the metamorphic version of limestone. Some kinds of metamorphic rock, such as gneiss, are suitable for mortared stone projects, though they are difficult to shape with a hammer; dense types, such as marble, are more commonly used for cut-stone projects such as monuments and countertops.

Within these three main categories are many kinds of stone used in mortared stonework. The list below describes some of the types you're likely to find at a stone yard. The list is by no means all-inclusive, nor is it a recommendation of what kind of stone you should use, but merely a reference to help you get a feel for the kind of stone you might want to look for. Your local stone yards are likely to have some kinds that aren't listed here, and may well not have some of the types I've mentioned. But this should give you a general idea of the range you're likely to find.

Argillite is a metamorphic form of shale and is usually black or dark brown. Because it's soft and can be easily carved with metal tools and polished, it's used as a sculptural material. For building, it's usually cut into rectangular or square shapes and used as block stone, or sometimes flagstone.

Gneiss is a banded metamorphic rock, usually made of the same components that are characteristic of its non-metamorphic parent, granite (described below). It varies in color and has a rustic surface quality, which makes a great building stone for thick veneers and retaining walls. In nature, it's often found on craggy slopes and in fields.

Granite is a common coarse-grained, light-colored, hard igneous rock consisting mainly of quartz, feldspar, and mica. It's often quarried or cut into blocks for monuments and buildings. As I've already mentioned, granite is difficult to trim and manipulate with a hammer and chisel, so it's a good choice for rustic stonework that doesn't require a crisp geometric look, such as a cabin foundation or a solid-stone column. Granite can also be used for building retaining walls, freestanding walls, and thick veneers.

Granite

Sandstone

Limestone is a common sedimentary rock consisting mostly of calcium carbonate. Limestone is soft and is very user friendly. It's great for formal, chiseled stonework, such as veneers, fireplaces, and chimneys. Avoid using limestone that's very soft and deteriorated, as it will break down and weaken the stonework.

Quartz is a very hard mineral found worldwide in many different types of rocks, notably sandstone and granite. Varieties of quartz include agate, chalcedony, flint, opal, and rock crystal. You'll often find chunks of quartz in piles of granite, or the granite itself may have large veins of quartz. The quartz is white or a pale color. In either case, avoid such rock—quartz is extremely difficult to manipulate with a hammer or chisel.

Quartzite is a rock formed from the metamorphism of quartz sandstone. Comprised mostly of quartz, it too is extremely dense and difficult to shape.

Sandstone is a sedimentary rock formed by the consolidation and compaction of sand and held together by a natural cement, such as silica. Sandstone is an exceptional choice for any stone project. It is easy to trim, break, and shape, and it can be found at most stone yards. Combine long, horizontal pieces of sandstone with a small percentage of fieldstones that match in color for a nice stone pattern.

Slate is a fine-grained metamorphic rock that splits into thin, smooth-surfaced layers. This stone has surface qualities similar to flagstone. In addition to serving as a handsome stone for patios and walkways, it's used for countertops and, less commonly than in the past, for roofing.

Stone Yard Lingo

Before you begin your project and head down to your local stone yard, familiarize yourself with the language of stonemasonry. Knowing the language will make your transactions with suppliers much smoother and easier.

Boulders

Aggregate stone is crushed, quarried stone, such as pea gravel and gravel used in concrete mixtures. Aggregate is also used in concrete for footings and is used for drainage behind retaining walls.

Ashlar is quarried stone that has been cut into geometric shapes and laid in regular patterns with uniform mortar joints. Ashlar stone was used in the construction of many old buildings as an alternative to brick and is still widely used for veneers on institutional buildings.

Boulders, as you undoubtedly know, are large rounded masses of rock lying on the surface of the ground or embedded in the soil. In stone yards, boulders are most often sold as landscape elements, although limestone and sandstone boulders can be broken into smaller pieces with a sledgehammer and used in walls and thick veneer stonework.

Crushed stone is small, quarried stone such as pea gravel. It's used in concrete for footings and for water drainage behind retaining walls.

Dimensional stone

Fieldstones

Culls are stones that can't be used in any project because they're too hard, they can't be manipulated, or they have an unusual shape or color. Quartz is often culled from a batch of granite not only because it's hard to work with, but also because it's a different color and stands out like a sore thumb in a wall or other structure. If you're building a wall with long, horizontal, flat stones, you'll also want to cull any round or egg-shaped stones from the pile.

Dimensional stone, also known as "cut stone," is material that has been sawn to particular dimensions. These include step treads, polished granite and marble, fireplace hearthstones and lintels, and wall capstones.

Dressed stone is any stone with a specific texture or pattern cut into the stone's face with a chisel or hammer by a stonemason.

Face stones. "Face" refers to the side of the stone chosen by the stonemason to be exposed on both horizontal and vertical surfaces. Shiners and fieldstones are sometimes referred to in stone yards as "face stones."

Fieldstones are usually sold in their unaltered form, just as they were found either lying on the surface of a field or embedded in the soil. Fieldstones can be used in walls, as stepping stones, and as pavers. Fieldstones are also called "shiners" or "face stones" and are sold in small, medium, and large sizes at most stone yards.

Flagstone is a hard, stratified stone that splits into flat pieces. Flagstones can be used for patios and sidewalks, as pavers, and as capstones and hearthstones. They usually range in thickness from 1 to 3 inches.

Face stones

Flagstone

Gravel

Quarried stones

Gravel is small, crushed stone. It's great for drainage behind retaining walls or beneath patios for fill. It's also used in concrete mixtures for footings and slabs.

Laydowns is the term sometimes used to refer to flat stones that are stacked in horizontal courses in stone structures.

Quarried stone is stone that's been broken or blasted from large pieces of bedrock in a quarry. Other than fieldstones and creek or river stones, most stone at the stone yard is quarried.

Quoins are cut cornerstones used for columns, wall ends, window corners, and door openings. Most quoins are literally cut, or sawed, into a blocklike shape and are used to form the outer corner of a wall. They're usually different in size and texture from the other blocks in the wall.

Riprap is small to medium-sized stone found at stone quarries. This stone is usually inexpensive and is perfect for backfilling retaining walls or solid stone columns.

River stones are stones that have been rounded on their edges over time by the force of water. River stones are difficult to manipulate with a hammer, so you have to work with them pretty much as they are. When used correctly, they make beautiful fireplaces, veneers, and columns.

Rock (and stone). Strictly speaking, "rock" refers to any naturally formed solid material from the earth's crust or from petrified matter. "Stone" suggests a smaller piece of rock, or rock that has been shaped for a particular purpose, such as a cornerstone or keystone, or by a force of nature, as is the case with river stone. It's perfectly okay, however, to use "rock" and "stone" pretty much interchangeably; just about everybody does.

River stones

Rubble sticks

Rubble stones

Veneer stones

Rubble sticks (pronounced "rooble" for some reason) are long, horizontal stones used for building stone veneers and mantel supports. They make nice, natural corners and are perfect for columns, wall ends, and mantel supports.

Rubble stones (pronounced more logically, as in Barney Rubble) are rough broken stones, also referred to as "rough stone," that are used for backfill in mortared stonework. Make sure you specify what size rubble stone you're looking for. Size terms vary among quarries and stone yards, so it's best just to describe, or show an example of, the size you want.

Veneer stones are sold as thick veneer stones or thin veneer stones. Thin veneer stones are usually 1 to 2 inches thick and are stuck broad face out to the wall, creating a thin veneer that is as thick as the stones and the thin layer of mortar used to stick the stones to the wall. Thick veneer stones are usually 3 to 5 inches thick and are stacked, creating a veneer 6 to 8 inches thick with stone and mortar.

Finding the Right Stone for Your Project

Spending time finding the right stone will make you feel better about the work in progress as well as the completed job. When looking for stone, there are many variables you should consider: color, texture, user-friendliness, and cost are just a few.

I recommend that you make several trips to your local stone yards or stone suppliers before you make any final decisions. Look at the photos of mortared stonework in magazines, books, and catalogues, and find a stone and pattern that you like. Take the pictures with you when you go stone shopping, and try your best to find a close match.

Stone yards differ in the ways they operate. Stone is almost always sold by weight unless you buy cut stone, which is sometimes sold by the piece. Some yards arrange their products by category—such as wall stone,

veneer, flagstone, and landscaping stone, each in its own area—while others are less organized. In most cases, the stone itself is stacked on a pallet and enclosed in a wire basket or wrapped in plastic, with a label naming the stone and identifying its weight and price. Often, the pallets contain 1 to 2 tons of stone. If you need only half a basket or pallet of stones, ask before you remove any from a pallet. Some yards don't allow you to purchase a partial pallet.

If there's more than one stone supplier in your area, compare prices and the quality of stone. Some stone yards that sell stone in baskets or on pallets stack good stone on top and around the edges of the basket, and put bad stone or culls in the middle. Pay attention to what you're buying.

Some stone suppliers sell loose stone as well. If you find loose stone, it's a good idea to handpick at least some of your own stone for your project. This takes more time and may also cost a bit more (stone yards often charge a handpicking fee in addition to the usual per-ton price) but you'll end up with better capstones, cornerstones, and other specialty stones such as mantel supports and hearthstones. It's usually worth the extra time and expense. Stone yards that offer loose stone usually have scales for weighing the loose stone you decide to buy. Some scales are located directly on loaders and others are drive-on scales.

Stone suppliers will not always have the type of stone you want, but if you plan ahead they'll probably be able to find what you're looking for and order it in advance. If you do find exactly what you want, go ahead and buy it even if you can't get it to the site right away. Stone sells quickly, and there are plenty of masons out there looking for the same thing you are. Stone yards will sometimes hold stone for several weeks. Most stone yards will deliver stone to you, but some don't—in which case you may need to rent a truck for hauling the stone to your site.

Gathering Stone

Some of the best stone you'll ever find is that which has already passed through the hands of a mason to build a now-abandoned chimney, fireplace, foundation, or wall. This stone is attractively weathered and has probably already been chiseled and shaped, which reduces the amount of work you have to do. I've actually taken down old stonework and numbered the stones so I'd know which were used for corners, caps, etc.

Just make sure that you obtain permission from the owner before removing any stone from someone else's property. Taking stone from private property without permission is illegal and can result in serious fines.

How Much Stone Will You Need?

Estimating the amount of stone you'll need for a given project isn't as difficult as it might seem. In general, for projects with vertical surfaces such as walls and fireplaces, 1 ton of stone equals approximately 30 square feet of stonework, unless you're exposing the large faces of fieldstones. In that case, 1 ton of stone will yield almost twice that area. To calculate the amount of stone you'll need, determine the square feet of the stonework by multiplying the length by the width, or height, including the capstones. Divide the resulting square footage by 30 to get the number of tons to buy.

For example, if your column is 4 feet tall and 2 feet wide on each side, each side will be 8 square feet. Multiply 8 times 4 (the number of sides), and you get 32 square feet. For the cap, multiply the length by the width: 2 times 2 equals 4 square feet. The total square footage for the project, then, is 36. With columns, you should always buy a little extra. This will give you plenty of corners and nice caps to choose from. Some pallets are sold with 1½ tons. This amount would be perfect. If a pallet has only 1 ton, I recommend buying two pallets. You can always use the extra for landscaping.

When estimating the amount of flagstone you'll need for paving a horizontal surface such as a walkway or patio, figure about 120 to 140 square feet per ton for 1-inch flagstone, sometimes referred to as regular flagstone at stone yards, and 70 to 80 square feet for thicker flagstone up to 3 inches. I don't recommend using thin flagstone; it's brittle and breaks easily when set with a mallet.

About Manufactured Stone

Manufactured stone is quickly becoming a popular alternative to natural stone for thin veneer, or "stick-on," mortared stonework. The reasons for its popularity are simple. Though most brands aren't much cheaper than natural stone, the actual installation requires less material and labor, and it doesn't take artistic talent to make it look good. Made of varying combinations of Portland cement, crushed stone, and pigments, the products are cast from molds made from real stone of various shapes and sizes and are finished to closely replicate natural colors and textures.

Manufactured stone is considerably lighter than natural stone and therefore needs less structural support while natural stone veneers need a solid foundation with enough protruding ledge to support the stone itself. Also, natural stone often has to be worked so that the next stone will rest solidly on top of it. If you're formally shaping the stone, each piece must be hammered and chiseled to fit tightly against the others. With manufactured stone, on the other hand, you can only hammer the stones very lightly because of their brittle qualities. They're designed for you to pick them right out of the box, apply mortar to the back, and stick them to the wall. In applications that require you to make them fit tightly together, you use an angle grinder with a diamond blade to shape them. They're much easier to cut than natural stone. Manufactured stone can be applied to block, brick, stucco, or a wood-sheathed wall. Both the jointed style and dry-stack style can be achieved using it.

Is there a visible difference between manufactured and natural stone veneers? Some say that good manufactured stone is virtually indistinguishable from the real thing; others say that nothing can replace the look and feel of natural stone, with each piece unique, shaped by the hand of a mason. I suggest that you take a look at both kinds of stone before you decide which might be right for your veneer project. Check with local stone and building supply companies; many have displays or catalogues showing various styles and colors of manufactured stone, and they may also be able to tell you where you can find some actual installations to look at, too. If you decide to use manufactured stone, more detailed instructions can be found on page 92.

Cornerstone

General Stonemason Terms

Capstones

Capstones are the uppermost stones on a wall or column that are laid horizontally over the top, often with a slight overhang and pitch to shed water.

Cornerstones are stones at the corner of a building, column, or wall end uniting two intersecting walls. The two faces usually form to make a 90° angle.

Courses are the horizontal layers of stones in stonework.

Joint refers to the gap or mortared area between adjacent stones in a stone structure. Horizontal joints run between courses, and vertical joints run between stones in each course. Mortar is visible in the joints of jointed-style stonework and on horizontal surfaces such as flagstone patios and wall capstones. I try to keep such joints no larger than 1 inch, and in most cases just $\frac{1}{2}$ to $\frac{3}{4}$ inch. I've found that stonework looks best if mortar joints are consistent. In dry-stack-style work, visible mortar is raked, or scratched out of the joints.

Plug

Running joint

Shiner

Plugs, or chinking stones, are small stones used to fill in the gaps between larger stones. Stonework looks much better with fewer plugs; however, plugs look better than large holes in dry-stack stonework.

Running joint refers to the joints in the courses of stonework that fall along the same vertical line. These joints need to be avoided as they create weak spots in the stonework.

Shims are small, flat pieces of stone used to fill gaps or level up stones.

Shiners are large face stones, such as fieldstones, in the vertical surface of stonework. I also use shiners with flat surfaces and smooth edges for caps on columns, retaining walls, freestanding walls, and sometimes hearths.

Stretchers are stones with long, horizontal faces that are usually laid on top of smaller stones to interrupt vertical, or running, joints.

Wedges are small, tapered stones used to level larger stones. To find wedges, simply look on the ground where you've chipped stones. Manipulating the faces of larger stones creates great wedges.

Wedge

Making Mortar

You can't create mortared stonework without mortar, of course, and making the right mortar—that is, mortar with the proper consistency, strength, and flexibility for the project at hand—is extremely important. You want the right consistency so that the material will spread easily but still have enough body to stay in place and support the stone without sagging while the mortar cures. You want the right strength so that all of your hard work won't be undone the instant someone leans on your column or sits on your retaining wall. You want enough flexibility in the mortar to allow it to absorb everyday loads and to expand and contract in response to changing temperatures without cracking or breaking apart.

Depending on the project, mortar can make up from 20 to 50 percent of the total volume of a stone structure. Mortar's primary function is to hold the stones together and bond them to a surface, but it also fills voids, seals out water, anchors metal ties and other fasteners, and can serve as an important visual element.

Making mortar right is essential, in other words. Making it wrong can threaten the structural integrity and appearance of your project.

Cement, Concrete, and Mortar

The terms cement, concrete, and mortar are sometimes used more or less interchangeably, but that's not quite right: although they're interrelated, each is distinctly different. To help you avoid confusing the terms, here are the differences. *Cement* is a binder, usually made of some combination of crushed limestone and clay, that hardens when mixed with water. *Portland cement,* the type of cement most commonly used today, is made by crushing, heating, and then finely grinding a mixture of calcium and silica (usually in the form of limestone, sand, and clay) and various other mineral-based substances such as aluminum and/or iron. Portland cement is *hydraulic;* when mixed with water, it doesn't harden by drying out, but changes chemically to a solid even if underwater.

Cement is seldom used by itself. Instead, it's mixed with gravel, sand, and water to make *concrete.* Modern concretes are mixed in varying proportions of Portland cement, sand, and gravel, depending on the strength required and the intended use.

Mortar has many of the characteristics of concrete, but is smoother and stickier and is made without gravel by mixing masonry cement (and/or Portland cement) with sand and water. *Masonry cement* itself is a mixture of Portland cement plus additional lime in proportions that vary according to the particular type of masonry cement, each of which offers different properties:

Type M has a very high compressive strength of 2,500 psi and is used primarily for masonry below grade or in contact with the earth, such as foundations and driveways.

Type N has a medium compressive strength of 750 psi and is considered a general-purpose mortar mix for both exterior and interior load-bearing installations.

Type O is rich in lime and has a low compressive strength of 350 psi. It's recommended primarily for above-grade, non-load-bearing stonework.

Type S has a high compressive strength of 1,800 psi but is also flexible and is suitable for both below- and above-grade work. It can be used for thin-veneer, stick-on stonework, and in combination with additional Portland cement for both exterior and interior stonework. Type S is also used in block and brickwork.

Mortar Mix Recipes

Premixed mortar, which includes sand, Portland cement, and masonry cement in one bag, is available and can be cost-effective for small jobs, such as any project less than 10 square feet. If your job is larger, I recommend mixing your own. You'll notice some of these recipes are the same—the difference is in the amount of water you add. I can't tell you just how much water to add because it will vary with each batch you make, but I describe how to determine the amount of water you need in the sidebar Checking for Consistency on page 45.

Mortar Mix for Dry-Stack Style

· *1 part Portland cement*
· *1 part type S masonry cement*
· *7 parts sand*
· *Water*

This is the mortar recipe I recommend for dry-stack thick veneer and dry-stack solid-stone projects.

Mortar Mix for Jointed Style

· *1 part Portland cement*
· *3 1/2 parts sand*
· *Water*

This is the mortar recipe I recommend for jointed-style thick-veneer and jointed-style solid-stone projects.

Mortar Mix for Horizontal Flagstone and Grout

· *1 part Portland cement*
· *3 1/2 parts sand*
· *Water*

This is the mortar recipe I recommend for horizontal flag-stone projects. Use this same recipe to make grout. For dry grout, use less water than you would for flagstone mortar. For wet grout, use more water than you do for flagstone mortar.

Mortar Mix for Stick-On and Thin Veneers

· *1 part type S masonry cement*
· *1 part sand*
· *Water*

This is the mortar recipe I recommend for stick-on and thin-veneer projects.

Mixing Mortar

Electric and gas-powered mortar mixers are great to have for large jobs when you'll need to mix a lot of batches in one day. You can rent a power mixer fairly inexpensively by the day or week. If you choose to do so, get a model with gear reduction and a large engine; they're a little more costly, but are also stronger and get the job done faster.

However, for most small projects that involve mixing just one or a few batches, mixing your mortar by hand is more practical and cost-efficient. True, it's also physically harder, but no more so than lifting heavy stones!

Tools Needed

For manually mixing mortar you'll need a 6-cubic-foot wheelbarrow or mortar pan. I use a heavy-duty wheelbarrow, which is more durable and easy to maneuver around the site (photo 1). After I mix mortar in the wheelbarrow or pour the mortar from the mixer into it, I work directly out of the wheelbarrow, depending on how close I can get it to the stonework. If your project is too tall to reach by hand, you'll also need some 5-gallon buckets to transfer the mortar onto scaffolding.

A square point shovel is the standard tool for shoveling mortar and sand into the mixing container, and for the mixing itself. Some people prefer mixing with a mortar hoe, which is a wide hoe with one or two holes in the blade.

You'll also need a water hose with a spray nozzle for cleaning mortar off the shovels and out of the wheelbarrows. If the temperature is below freezing during any portion of the day, use some type of mortar antifreeze to prevent the mortar from freezing before it cures.

The Process

Unless you're making mortar for stick-on stonework, never make more than one batch at a time—which among stonemasons is considered to be a total of one-half bag of cement plus whatever sand is required. There are several reasons for not making more at once. Your wheelbarrow will not last very long if you continually overload it; it'll be difficult to push, and the mortar will get too dry before you can use it all. (Mortar for stick-on stonework is a different matter. Because there is so much less sand and generally more water in the mix, you can use a full bag of cement in the mix.)

To make one batch of dry-stack style mortar mix, you'll need one-fourth bag of Portland cement and one-fourth bag of type S masonry cement. A fourth of a bag is equivalent to about two square point shovelfuls of cement.

Buying and Opening Bags of Cement

When you purchase bags of cement, look out for tears in the bag. Tears or holes will make the bag difficult to open and will create a mess. Don't buy damaged bags. Make sure, too, that the mortar in the bag isn't hard. If mortar is old or has gotten wet in storage either from direct contact with water or by absorbing the moisture in humid air, it will have hard lumps in it. If the bag isn't somewhat pliable, it may be no good. Always cover the bags at the end of each day and stack them on a pallet.

To open a bag of cement, use a knife or the blade of a shovel to cut the bag in half. Then take your hand and lift the bag from the bottom along the split seam. When both halves are sitting upright, use a knife or your hand to cut the back side. This will divide the bag into two halves. Most batches of mortar require a total of one half of a bag of cement, whether Portland, masonry cement, or a combination of both.

Set a 6-cubic-foot wheelbarrow or mortar pan on flat ground near the sand and cement. Shovel half the amount of sand in first (photo 2), followed by all of the cement, followed by the other half of the sand.

Now, before adding any water, mix the sand and cement together until the combined ingredients are uniform in color. The easiest way to do this is to take your shovel or hoe and slice small sections of the mix like you're slicing bread, pulling each slice toward you one at a time to the near end of the wheelbarrow or pan. When it's all to one side, move to the other side and chop and pull small sections toward you in that direction. It may take several passes before the mortar mix color is consistent. (This blending process is much easier when there are two people at opposite ends, each taking a turn pulling the mix toward their end.)

When the mixture is uniform in color, slowly add water (photo 3) and use the same chopping technique to mix all the water into the mixture. Make sure you chop the mortar in thin slices to get out all of the lumps (photo 4). Be sure, too, that your hoe or shovel touches the bottom of the pan or wheelbarrow with each chop, so that the mortar on the bottom is mixed.

If you need to add more water, pour it in small increments to prevent the mix from becoming too soupy, a situation that can happen all too easily. There is really no way to measure exactly how much water a given batch will need, because the dampness of the sand and the absorption rate of different amounts of mortar varies.

If the mortar mix becomes too wet, slowly add the same ratio of sand and mortar until you get it right. Make sure all of the sand and mortar in the corners of the container and on the bottom are thoroughly mixed. It may take five or six sessions of back-and-forth slicing before the batch is completely mixed.

About Sand

Sand for making mortar should be sharp-edged and relatively coarse. Most building supply stores sell the material in bulk as "builder's sand." Finer-grade sand such as sandbox sand is okay in a pinch for small projects, but in general should be avoided. For dry-stack style projects, I often use river sand if it's clean. Check the sand before you buy it to make sure it's free of large pebbles, sticks, or any other type of small debris. Sand can be found at most masonry supply stores in bulk and is usually sold by the cubic yard or by weight. When you're not using it, keep your sand covered with a tarp or plastic to keep it dry and free of debris.

Checking for Consistency

Mixing mortar to the right consistency for the purpose at hand—in other words, adding the right amount of water—is something of an art. Below are some general guidelines for the various types of mortar used in stonework.

Dry-Stack Style Mortar

For dry-stack style stonework, the mortar should be wet enough to spread with a trowel, but not wet enough to seep over the edges of the stones. It needs to be wet enough to pack behind the stones and not leave a wet residue on your hands, which will stain the stones when you pick them up. The mortar also needs to have some body so that it can support the stones when you pack behind them. Take a small handful of mortar and squeeze it; it should compress easily and feel sticky, but should also hold together and not leave a pasty film on your hand.

Jointed-Style Mortar

Mortar for jointed-style stonework needs to be somewhat drier; it should be slightly sticky but still crumbly. The best way to tell if it's wet enough is to pat a small amount softly into a ball with one hand and toss it into the air. It should stay in a ball, not crumble apart or fall to pieces. If it does, it might be too dry. Add a small amount of water. If it stains your gloves or leaves a lot of moisture on your hands after you pick it up, it's probably too wet.

Flagstone Mortar

If you're making mortar for flagstone, make it slightly wetter than dry-stack mortar. If you make it too soupy, your stones will shift and won't stay level. If it's too dry, the stones won't stick. Sometimes the best way to make flagstone mortar is by trial and error. After tapping the stone into place with a mallet, try to pull it off the mortar bed. If the stone is stuck, and doesn't shift from one side to the other, it's fine. If you can easily pull it off the mortar bed, it might be too dry.

Dry-Grout Mortar

Dry-grout mortar should be drier than flagstone mortar. Pat the mortar into a ball and toss it into the air. If it stays in a ball and doesn't leave a wet residue on your hands, it's usable. If it crumbles, add a little more water and mix it up. If it's too wet, it will leave a wet residue on your hands. Since you'll be using your hands to grout around the edges of the stones, you might stain them. Add a little more sand and cement. Note: If you add more sand and cement, make sure you add the same proportions so that the grout stays consistent in color.

Wet-Grout Mortar

It's hard to make wet grout too wet. Wet-grout mortar should be as wet as scratch-coat mortar and a little wetter than stick-on mortar. It should be wet enough that it easily comes out of the grout bag (similar to cake icing) but not so wet that it runs out over the surfaces of the stones. You want it to have enough body to stay in place once you apply it between the joints.

Stick-On Mortar

Stick-on mortar should be sticky and very wet. Because it's made with type S masonry cement, the texture is different than that of standard mortar mix. After you've made a batch, you don't want it so wet that water pools on top or around the edges. If so, it's too soupy. When applied to the back of the stone with a trowel, the mortar should stick to the back without dripping over the edges. Stick the stone to a vertical surface and hold it in place for 10 to 20 seconds. If it slides down the wall, it's probably too wet. If it falls off after five minutes, it's probably too dry.

Pattern & Style

What is it that makes one person prefer the look of jointed-style stonework and another dry-stack style? Why does one client lean toward a rustic look for her fireplace while another wants clean, formal lines?

I can't answer such questions because, a lot of the time, it seems to me it's just a matter of taste. I've analyzed a good deal of stonework and created countless projects with many different styles; some look like something I'd want on my own dream home and some look like an eyesore. I can't tell you what should or shouldn't appeal to you aesthetically, but I can offer a look at some of the different styles and patterns for mortared stonework and walk you through the process of achieving a look that's right for you.

Dry-stack style mimics the look of dry-laid stonework.

Styles of Stonework

There are different styles of mortared stonework, but, as I've mentioned before, the two main styles are dry-stacked and jointed. All of the projects in this book are done in one of these two styles. Let's look at these two styles in terms of design.

Dry-Stack Style

Dry-stack style stonework has no visible mortar joints; it mimics the look of nonmortared dry-laid stonework. The differences between the dry-stack style and the jointed style have more to do with aesthetics than structural integrity. If done correctly, both styles are equally strong.

Jointed-style stonework can look formal or informal.

To my mind, the dry-stack style looks more organic and rustic than the jointed style, especially when chiseling and manipulating the stone's faces are minimized. Perhaps because I live in a rural, mountainous area, my clients tend to prefer the look of dry-stacked-style stonework. To enhance the rustic appearance of this style, I limit the amount I trim the faces of the stones, leave the natural, weathered edges exposed, and let veneers fluctuate in depth. I sometimes let dry-stack-style veneer vary anywhere from 5 to 9 inches in depth to create the uneven, old-timey look of a chimney on a 200-year-old cabin. The dry-stack style can work in many different locations and applications. It's a great style to use on foundation walls, fireplaces, columns, interior walls, freestanding walls, and retaining walls.

Jointed Style

When I think of my favorite stone structures that have survived for hundreds of years, images of medieval castles and stone churches in Europe, as well as countryside stone houses in France, come to mind. But jointed-style stonework can also be used to great effect in contemporary settings, whether it's on the foundation of a modern house or on a fireplace. It can give structures a modern or urban feel, and squared ashlar stone with mortar joints works well when you want a formal look.

The visible mortar joints of this style play both a functional and an aesthetic role. Remember, as you lay jointed-style stone, to keep the thickness of your joints consistent throughout the entire project—usually ¼ to ¾ inch thick between each stone, both vertically and

The mortar in the jointed style plays an aesthetic, as well as a functional, role.

horizontally. A 1-inch-thick joint is acceptable if you're using large stones, but in general try to make the joints as small as possible and keep them consistent. You also need to pay special attention to the way you finish the joints. Before they dry, strike them back with a stick or a tuck pointer or any other tool with parallel edges. This will give them a uniform look. If there are pockets or voids or pieces of debris in the joints, repair them with fresh mortar before they dry. Don't scratch the mortar back if it's too wet—this will stain the edges of the rocks.

I usually don't use the jointed style if I'm laying a lot of thin, horizontal stones. I think this takes away from the stones and draws too much attention to the mortar joints. Also, the grouting process takes longer and is more tedious between small stones. I do prefer the jointed style if I am using ashlar stone that's uniform in color. When smooth-faced stones that are all one color are dry stacked, you tend to lose sight of the natural

shapes of the stones. A slightly different colored grout will provide relief around each of the stones and will accentuate each one. Lay stone with the jointed style if you're using large stones or integrating large stones into your pattern. The mortar joints will accentuate the stones rather than take away from them.

Striking back jointed-style joints with a tuck pointer gives them a uniform, finished look.

Scramble pattern on a vertical surface

Patterns

When we talk about pattern in stonework, we're talking about the order in which stones are arranged. You can lay your stone (especially ashlar stone that's regular in shape) in very set patterns. This tends to give the stonework a formal look. I prefer a more natural look, so I employ a more holistic approach. I let the individual shapes and colors of the stones help me decide just how I should arrange them. This doesn't result in a geometric pattern, but it does create what's called "rhythm" in the structure's design. This rhythm is a subtle thing, yet it has a real effect on the appearance of your final product.

Scramble Pattern

The best way to describe the scramble pattern is to imagine taking a flagstone patio and placing it vertically against a wall (photo above). The stones have no set pattern; they're just laid out in their random shapes. The scramble pattern doesn't necessarily reduce the amount of chiseling you do to each stone. In fact, it might require a little more work, especially if you minimize the amount of plugs and wedges you put into the stonework, and I do recommend keeping plugs and wedges at a minimum.

When buying stone for the scramble pattern, look for fieldstones with large and irregular faces. Since you'll have to chisel many of the stones to get them to fit together like a giant puzzle, try to buy sandstone or limestone, which is easier to cut. Granite and other dense stones will be difficult to work with. Because the scramble pattern is like putting a huge puzzle together, if you buy a large amount of stone, perhaps more than you need, you'll eventually find most of the right pieces. If not, you'll need to alter the shapes of your stones.

Both the jointed and dry-stack styles can be used for the scramble pattern. However, I recommend using the jointed style with this pattern so that you don't spend as much time chiseling the stones' edges.

Horizontal Stone Pattern

The horizontal stone pattern consists of primarily flat, horizontal stones stacked on top of each other. I recommend doing the dry-stacked style with this pattern. It looks better, it's easier to stack the stones, and you don't

have to tediously pack around each stone with mortar. It's important with this pattern to keep each stone level. If you do get one stone out of level, trim a little off the top or make up the difference with the next stone.

Flat, horizontal stones are usually easy to find. Most stone suppliers carry stone that's perfect for stacking. Buy sandstone or limestone if your project requires a lot of corners. If it doesn't, any type of flat stone will work. This pattern is perfect for small projects such as veneered walls, fireplaces, and step risers.

Horizontal Stones with Random Fieldstones

This pattern consists of flat, horizontal stones with randomly placed fieldstones. I usually do a mixture of 80 per-

cent horizontal stones and 20 percent fieldstones. This pattern can be done in both the jointed and dry-stacked styles.

Since so much chiseling is involved in fitting horizontal stones between larger field-stones, I recommend using a soft stone, such as sandstone or lime-stone. With this pattern, I find that stones with 90° angles and slightly obtuse and acute angles are much easier to work with. Avoid odd-shaped triangles and round stones, as these are hard to work with and will make the stonework look sloppy.

Patterns for Horizontal Surfaces

My favorite pattern for a flagstone patio or walkway is the scramble pattern (photo below). The other option is to use cut flagstone and develop some kind of formal pattern, but in my opinion, such patterns tend to look too contrived and resemble tile, which I prefer to see in bathrooms and on countertops.

When choosing the color of stone to use, keep in mind the colors of your house or the landscape.

Choosing a Color

Although it comes as a surprise to some, color is one of the most important considerations in stonework. In fact, the first thing you should do before you choose a pattern and style is visit the stone yard and choose the color of stone you want, based on the colors of your house, the landscape, or the environment surrounding your stonework. Most building stone that's consistent in color comes in various sizes, so don't worry about size at first.

You don't necessarily need to match the stonework with its surroundings, but you don't want too much of a contrast either. One of the first things a visitor will notice is a stone fireplace in your living room or the stone veneer on your new house. Don't overdo it with bright, contrasting colors. It's best to stay neutral with the stone if you're unsure about a color. Stonework is very difficult to remove once it's mortared.

My favorite stone colors are brown and gray or a combination of the two on just about any type of stonework. Most stones, whether they're flagstones or fieldstones, are dirty when you purchase them. When you spray them off with water, you'll see their natural face colors. This color is usually different than the raw color inside after you chip away the face with a hammer. If you want a weathered, natural look, minimize trimming. If you want to expose the brighter interior of the stones, trim as much as you can.

If your stonework will be in a room that's poorly lit or painted a dark color or in a shady spot in the landscape, use stones that are light in color, such as tan or light grey. If you prefer a sharp contrast, use stones with a lot of color. Some flagstones come in pink, orange, yellow, and tan, but these are my least favorites. If the area around the stonework has earthtone colors, such as green or brown, stick with similar colored flagstones, only use slightly different shades.

If all this color talk has succeeded only in confusing you, remember that it's hard to go wrong with a neutral, moderately colored stone. You can bet this will look good and almost always blend in with its environment. Whatever color you choose, keep in mind that stone always weathers and turns somewhat darker over time.

River stones

Horizontal stacked stones

Texture

Stone Shapes

How different shapes of stone look in relation to one another is yet another thing to consider when choosing stones. River stones, for instance, don't go very well with horizontal stacked stones. They look better with other river stones. And since river stones are irregular in shape, you're limited in how you put them together, unless you want to chisel each stone into a particular shape, and I don't recommend that since these stones are difficult to manipulate.

A good rule of thumb is to use stones within each pattern that have the same edges. If your long, flat stones have sharp edges, incorporate fieldstones or other flat stones with sharp edges into the pattern. Always pay attention to the aesthetic qualities of all the stones in each pattern. If your favorite stone has round edges, but you want to add the color of another type of stone, use a stone that also has round edges.

Texture

The natural faces of the stones give stonework texture, and this texture tends to make stone structures look natural—older and more rustic. Stones that have been cut at the stone yard are often very smooth and unnatural looking. When working with this kind of stone I sometimes use a blunt chisel to trim away the edges a bit and add some texture. With uncut stones, I prefer to leave as much texture on the stones as possible at all times. Stones aren't perfect in nature, so why try to make them that way? Whenever a homeowner points out a favorite stone in a project, it always seems to be a stone's face that was left natural, devoid of any hammer or chisel marks.

I think one reason dry-stack style textured stonework is so popular is that it blends new homes and projects with old landscapes so well. With a stone wall, this stonework adds a natural element to garden or flowerbeds; and with a fireplace, it brings a hint of the outdoors to your living room or porch. If the natural look is what you're after, it makes sense to leave stones the way they're found in nature.

The large cornerstone makes this wall look strong.

Stone Sizes

Blending larger stones with small and medium-size stones will give the stonework a stronger look. But try to avoid combining very large stones with very small, thin stones. Large stones look good at the base of a stone structure, making it appear as though it's sitting on a strong, solid foundation. If you're using a lot of horizontal stones, blend large, long horizontal stones into the pattern and on the corners to make the stonework look stronger.

In general, using large stones in large surface areas and small stones in small surface areas will make everything look proportional. If your fireplace is only 5 feet tall, don't use anything larger than medium-size stones or you'll find yourself cramped for space when laying the jams, under the mantel, and up the sides. Using small stones in smaller spaces also means you'll have less trimming to do.

Unless you have a helper, I don't recommend ever using very large stones, especially if you'll be working on scaffolding. However, if you're doing a large wall veneer or fireplace, larger stones will make the stonework look stronger and perhaps anchored. This might be a good time to call on that friend that owes you a favor. If you're using scaffolding, trim stones on the ground before you lift them onto the scaffolding.

Raked joint

Joint Styles

Grouting techniques and joint styles play an important role in the look of mortared stonework. With the flush style (figure 1), mortar joints are raked flush with the faces of the stones. I think it makes the stonework look older, more rustic, and perhaps stronger. This look can be achieved with tuck pointers, trowels, or anything with a straight edge. The rougher the joint is, the more rustic it will look. Laying this style is fast and allows you to use irregular stones, since the edges will be filled with mortar.

Another popular mortar joint is the raked style (photo above and figure 1), where joints are recessed from the faces of the stones, preferably ¼ to ¾ inch. This type of mortar joint tends to look more formal. Joints are raked with either a tuck pointer or a tool that's the same width as the joints.

A joint style that was used often in old jointed stonework is called a rope, or bead joint (see top photo, next page, and figure 1). A tool was used to outline a raised strip, about

FIGURE 1: **Joint Styles**

Flush

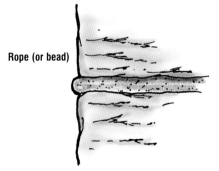

Raked

Rope (or bead)

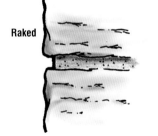

Rope joint

½ inch thick, in the middle of the mortar joint throughout the stonework. The joints have more of a connected appearance with this style, but I think this style takes the focus away from the stones and puts it on the mortar joints.

I usually like to use the raked style of joints; I recommend you pay attention to the joints used in stonework you admire, and then experiment a bit to see what style of joint appeals to you and works best with both your project and your stone. Whatever style joint you use, your stonework will look best when the joints are small, consistent, and neat.

There might be situations where you want to use mortar joints to accentuate the shape of each stone. Mortar joints are especially good at doing this if the grout is a different shade than the stone (bottom photo). A lighter grout with dark stones and a darker grout with light-colored stones will offer a pleasing contrast. Most grout is some shade of gray. For a darker gray, use only a Portland cement and sand mix. For a lighter grout, add type S mortar mix to the Portland cement and sand mix. Remember that mortar will lighten a little when it cures, so you might want to make a little and let it dry before you make your final decision.

The entry columns above were built with contrasting mortar.

Mortared Stone Basics

In previous chapters you learned about tools, stones, mortar, and the patterns and styles used in mortared stonework. You're probably itching to get out there and build, and this chapter will get you started. Here, I walk you through the basics, the general principals that apply to nearly any mortared stone project.

Preparing the Work Site

Whether you're laying a flagstone patio or walkway, veneering a fireplace, or constructing a pair of columns, you want to make sure your work site is prepared. By doing so, you'll save yourself a lot of time and frustration. The process of laying stone can be very rhythmic; once you get focused, the fewer distractions the better. Having the area cleared and all your tools and materials on site will prevent you from having to interrupt the process. Here are a few simple ways to get your workspace ready for stone.

Place materials close to the project for easy access.

Make sure the delivery truck can get close to the work site.

You want the mixer close to the project but not in the way.

A board makes a good ramp for a wheelbarrow.

Make Room for Materials

Be sure you have plenty of room for materials: stone, sand, mortar, mixer, hoses, buckets, etc. Also, clear your workspace of debris or other obstacles that might get in the way of wheelbarrows or foot traffic. You'll need plenty of space to work with stone, especially in your immediate work area. If stone is being delivered, you'll need a place for the truck to dump it or to unload pallets of stone, preferably as close to the work site as possible, so you won't have to move each stone very far.

If you're using a mixer, find a spot for it that's convenient but not in the way. A mixer requires a thorough rinsing after each batch of mortar, so have a long hose available. Locating the mixer near a downhill slope will make it easier to empty it after each rinse. Dump the sand and cement you'll be using close to the mixer so you won't have to carry it very far. Portland cement bags weigh almost 100 pounds each, so the less you have to carry them, the better. Stack the cement on a pallet so the bags on the bottom won't get wet, and remember to cover the stack with plastic at the end of each day.

If you're laying stone inside your house or on a porch, use ramps to transport wheelbarrows of stone and mortar over thresholds or steps. When you bring stones into the house, spread them out over the floor so that all the weight is evenly distributed. Heavy piles of stone in one spot have been known to fall through a floor! Spreading out the stone also lets you see what you have to work with.

Protecting Surfaces

Mortar is extremely difficult to remove. When grouting a patio or capstones or laying stone against trim (perhaps on the sides of a fireplace or a patio), you'll no doubt get mortar on finished surfaces. The best way to prevent this from happening is to use some type of tape for protection. A couple of strips of tape can be removed easily when the stonework is completed and will save a lot of unnecessary touch-ups. Just don't place the tape under the grouting area—you won't be able to remove it after the mortar cures. If you're laying stone on top of a finished floor or deck, protect the floors from flying stone chips. The best way to do this is to spread sheets of plastic over the surface of the floor and then spread a few sheets of plywood on top of the plastic. I recommend covering the entire floor of the room.

If you're building a fireplace on an unfinished floor or beside an unfinished wall, nail in place a piece of temporary trim, or "ground," that's the same thickness as the final trim or floor will be. This can be removed after you lay the stone and be replaced with permanent trim. I recommend nailing the ground into a stud, leaving part of the nail sticking out so that it will be easy to remove. Don't remove it until the mortar is cured.

Use tape to protect surfaces from mortar.

This temporary trim will be removed once the stonework is complete.

Lifting Heavy Objects

Stonework is taxing on your body. Whether you're lifting a heavy stone or pushing a wheelbarrow full of mortar, you should always take safety precautions. You'll load and unload heavy Portland cement bags and then empty them at your mixing station. Most batches of mortar require 14 shovels of sand. That's a lot of bending and maneuvering at one mixing session. For any stone project you pursue, you'll constantly move the stones around the site and your work station. If you're a perfectionist like me, you'll remove a stone from the wall several times before getting it the way you want it. Keep these safety tips in mind when it comes to lifting stones.

◆ You've probably heard the saying, *lift with your legs, not your back*. To do so, crouch down with your knees bent and your back straight; then use your leg muscles to lift the object while holding it close to your body.

◆ If you're going to carry the stone, hold it very close to you and keep your back straight while you're walking. Unless it's a very brittle stone, like thin flagstone, drop it instead of setting it on the ground. This will be much easier on your back. Don't drop stone on a wood floor or any type of finished surface.

◆ If a friend is helping you lift a stone, communicate about the direction you're going and the final resting spot for the stone.

◆ Whenever possible, avoid carrying heavy stones very far. Use carts, wheelbarrows, hand trucks, log rollers, or any other means to get them to the site. The less time you spend carrying heavy objects, the more energy you will have for the actual stonework. It's easier to navigate around the site if you leave enough room to walk, carry materials, and push a wheelbarrow. Plan ahead before you unload the stones.

Footing trench

Footings and Bases

The soil beneath a stone structure can sink, shift, and (in cold climates where the ground freezes) heave. Mortared stone structures are rigid, so if the ground beneath a stone wall moves, that wall might sink, crack, or even collapse. To prevent this from happening, vertical mortared stone structures (such as walls, columns, and benches) often need concrete footings (see figure 1) to spread the weight of the structure over the ground and to provide a solid barrier between the structure and the soil. Horizontal projects (such as walkways and patios) aren't in danger of collapsing, but they can—depending on soil conditions and climate—buckle, crack, or sink. The most durable mortared-stone paths and patios have stones set in a mortar bed on top of a concrete base, or "pad." Let's look at footings first; then I'll cover bases.

Smoothing the footing surface

FIGURE 1: **Footing for a Wall**

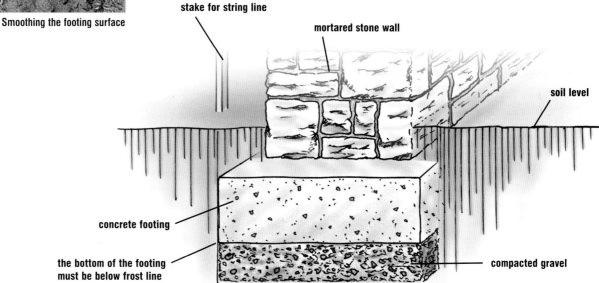

stake for string line

mortared stone wall

soil level

concrete footing

the bottom of the footing must be below frost line

compacted gravel

Footings

In this section, I'll teach you to make footings for a mortared-stone wall. In the individual projects, I'll tell you how to adapt these instructions to make footings for columns and benches. Building codes for footings are specific and vary depending on where you live. Requirements for one in an earthquake-prone area may well differ from those in a place where the ground freezes very deep each winter, so check with your local building officials before you begin. A building permit may also be required.

■ Determining the Size and Depth of a Footing

The size and depth of the footing required will depend on your climate, your soil conditions, and the height and weight of your wall. As a general rule, footings for structures 3 feet tall or less should be at least 8 inches wider than the stonework, or 4 inches wider on each side. For structures taller than that, footings should be nearly twice the width of the wall's thickness. The bottom of any footing should be below the frost line, and the concrete usually should be at least 8 inches deep. Your local building codes may specify an exact depth for your footing, so again, check with the building department before you build. If your soil is unstable or has poor drainage, you'll need to lay a 4- to 6-inch-deep layer of tamped gravel as a subbase before you pour your concrete footing.

■ Digging the Trench for a Footing

If your soil is soft, you'll need to build forms to hold the concrete. Drive stakes into the ground to mark the four corners of the footing; then stretch mason's line between the stakes to outline the edges of the footings. The trench for a footing that doesn't require formwork can be outlined with marking spray (photo 1). Keep in mind that the footing needs to be about 8 inches wider than the stonework. Dig the trench for your footing, remembering that its depth must accommodate not only the thickness of the footing but also any tamped gravel you may be adding (photos 2–4).

4

Remember, too, that you want the top of your footing to rest several inches below the soil's surface so it won't show once the stonework is completed. If your footing is on an incline, you might need to step up the trench so that the concrete doesn't run to the bottom of the slope, see Preparing a Footing on a Slope on page 109 for instructions.

Once the trench is dug, compact the soil with a hand compactor to prevent the footing from settling in the future. If your soil is dense enough to maintain its shape and hold the concrete, you can skip the next section and just follow the directions for mixing concrete and pouring the footing. However, if the soil is soft and loose, you'll need to build forms to contain the concrete.

■ Building Forms for a Footing

Figure 2 shows a typical formwork for a footing. Use 2x4s or 2x6s, depending on how deep the trench is, as form boards on each side of the trench. Drive stakes into the ground where each long two-by meets to hold the boards together. Use a string and line level to make sure the boards are level with each other. Fasten the long two-bys to each stake.

If you're building a footing for a wall that turns or curves, use strips of plywood instead of two-bys since they'll bend easier. If you use plywood, you'll need to add extra stakes so the sides won't bulge after you pour.

FIGURE 2: **Footing Formwork**

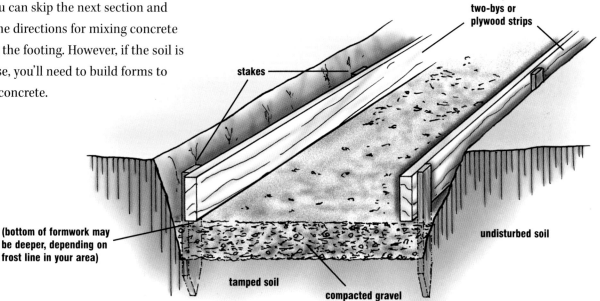

two-bys or plywood strips

stakes

(bottom of formwork may be deeper, depending on frost line in your area)

tamped soil

compacted gravel

undisturbed soil

■ Buying Concrete

Concrete consists of sand, Portland cement, and gravel. Depending on the amount of money you want to spend and the size of the job, you have three choices: You can buy bags of premixed concrete and simply add water, you can buy each individual ingredient and mix your own, or you can hire a concrete company to deliver concrete to you.

Consider purchasing premixed concrete in 60- or 80-pound bags and mixing in a wheelbarrow if your footing calls for less than ½ cubic yard of concrete. (See the sidebar Calculating the Amount of Concrete for a Footing to figure out how much concrete your footing will require.) For jobs requiring more than ½ cubic yard of concrete, you can usually save money (but not time) by buying the individual ingredients (Portland cement, sand, and gravel) and mixing your own. Whichever type you choose, you can also rent a gas or electric power mixer to help with the chore of mixing. It's basically a matter of weighing the expense of a power mixer versus the time and labor it takes to mix by hand. A power mixer will help ensure a more even mix.

For larger jobs, you may want to have wet concrete delivered. Check and see—sometimes the cost isn't that much more than buying the tools and ingredients to make your own.

■ Mixing Concrete

Portland cement is caustic, so before you begin, put on work gloves, safety glasses, and rubber boots. Also, clear the site of any debris so you have clear access to the trench. To hand mix your concrete, add the ingredients to a wheelbarrow and dry mix them first, using a shovel or mason's hoe, before adding any water. Once all the dry ingredients are thoroughly mixed, begin adding clean water, a little at a time. Determining the amount of water needed is more of an art than a science, but the best advice I can give you is to remember that you can always add more water, but you can't take excess water out! The end product should be a plastic mixture that's firm enough to hold peaks but levels out when you shake it with a hoe. A soupy or watery mix will result in weak concrete.

If you rent a power mixer, be sure to have someone knowledgeable at the rental company explain all its parts and how to operate it before you leave with it. Remember, too, that an electric mixer will require power at the site. In general, I mix the dry ingredients first, and then slowly add in water as the machine is mixing until I get the correct consistency.

Concrete Recipe

To make your own concrete for a footing, use 1 part Portland cement, 2 parts sand, and 3 parts small gravel. When it comes time to mix the ingredients in my wheelbarrow, this usually means 3 shovels of Portland cement, 6 shovels of sand, and 9 shovels of small gravel.

5

■ Pouring a Concrete Footing

Before you pour the concrete, brush any type of oil on the interior of the form boards (if you're using them) so they won't stick to the concrete. Use a hose to moisten any tamped gravel in the trench's bottom. Starting at one end of the trench, pour the concrete (photo 5) and spread it with a rake, hoe, or shovel so that it doesn't mound too much in one spot. Slice the concrete with the shovel to eliminate air pockets.

Use a piece of scrap lumber to level off, or "screed," the concrete with the top of the trench or form boards. Try to get the depth of the footing right, but don't worry about making the surface perfectly even. If you have a few small dips and uneven places on the top of the footing, you can make up for it later by adjusting the mortar bed beneath your stonework. Figure 5 on page 71 shows how to screed a concrete base for a patio. Use the same technique to screed the top of your concrete footing.

Calculating the Amount of Concrete for a Footing

To estimate the amount of concrete you'll need for a footing, first multiply your trench's or form's width by its depth in inches. Divide the answer by 144 to convert to square feet. Multiply that amount by the footing's length (in feet). This will tell you the square feet of concrete needed. Divide this number by 27 to determine the amount of cubic yards of concrete you'll need.

■ Raising a Footing with Blocks

In some situations, you may need to pour your footing deep below the soil's surface. There's no point in wasting expensive stone that won't be seen to fill the space; you can instead lay courses of 8-inch block on top of the footing until they reach just below the level of finished grade. An alternative would be to fill the trench with more concrete, but laying blocks is cheaper. To stack blocks, follow the instructions for laying block on page 72.

Bases

For horizontal projects, such as patios and walkways, you have three choices of bases for your stonework. If you live in an area where frost heave isn't a concern and you're building on stable soil, you can hollow out your patio or path area and mortar the stones directly on compacted soil or crushed gravel. Otherwise, you can use an existing concrete pad or walkway as your base, or, if you're up to the task, you can pour your own concrete pad. The first two methods are covered in the instructions for Patios and Walkways on page 152. I'll describe how to construct a concrete base here.

■ Laying Out and Excavating the Base

Use batter boards or marking spray to define your walkway or patio and to give you an idea of what the big picture will look like; for projects with curves, a garden hose or rope might work better. Remember to keep the width of a path constant—I recommend making most walkways between 3 and 4 feet wide.

Begin excavating, keeping in mind the following when it comes to determining the depth of your foundation: The general rule of thumb for laying flagstone on pads is to use 2- to 3-inch-thick flagstones, a 2- to 3-inch-thick

mortar bed for the flagstones, a 4-inch-thick concrete pad, and a few inches of crushed gravel beneath the concrete. The depth of your excavation will vary depending on the thickness of your stones and the density of the soil. If the soil is soft, you'll need to dig until you get to compacted soil, then you can add gravel to make up the difference.

Remember that once you pave the concrete base, its finished height will be higher, so plan accordingly. If your patio slab butts up against a door to the house, for instance, you'll need to make sure that the paved slab will still be lower than the floor of the house.

Loosen soil and small roots with a mattock (photo 1) and shovel. If the soil is rocky and contains large roots, you might need a pry bar and saw or an adz hoe. Use a shovel to remove the soil and square the sides of the trench to contain the concrete. As you excavate, you need to grade the site so that it slopes just the right amount to drain water properly (photo 2). This slope is known as the site's "pitch." See the sidebar Establishing a Base's Pitch for more information. Once you have the site properly excavated, add 3 inches of $\frac{1}{2}$- to $\frac{3}{4}$-inch gravel. Use a shovel to spread the gravel evenly, and then use a level to check that the gravel layer maintains the correct pitch.

Establishing a Base's Pitch

A base must slope just slightly so water doesn't puddle on it. This slope is also what keeps water from running into an adjacent building foundation. The standard slope, or "pitch," is 2 percent, or ¼ inch per linear foot. This means for every foot of surface, measured from the highest point to the lowest, the surface must slope ¼ inch downward. To calculate the overall pitch of your site, measure the distance from the edge where the patio should be the highest (near a house foundation, for instance) to the edge that should be the lowest. Multiply that length by ¼ to get the overall number of inches of pitch needed. For example, if your patio is 10 feet long, multiply ¼ by 10. The result, 2½ inches, is the pitch needed over a span of 10 feet. The surface at the highest point of your patio should be 2½ inches higher than the surface at the other end. To achieve this pitch, you'll need to grade your site, adding soil or skimming it away as necessary.

To establish the 2 percent pitch, first insert two stakes at what should be the high end of your patio (near the foundation, for instance) and two stakes at what should be the low end. Attach a taut string and line level to the stakes, leveling the string so the air bubble in the level rests in the center of the vial (see photo above). If you're using batter boards, you can attach the strings to these instead. Then adjust the string (see figure 3), so the level's bubble rests against the outer line on the vial, reflecting a 2 percent slope (or a ¼-inch drop per linear foot). When you excavate your site, use the sloped string as a guide (measuring from the string down to the base of the excavation), to make sure the floor is sloping correctly.

FIGURE 3: **Establishing Pitch**

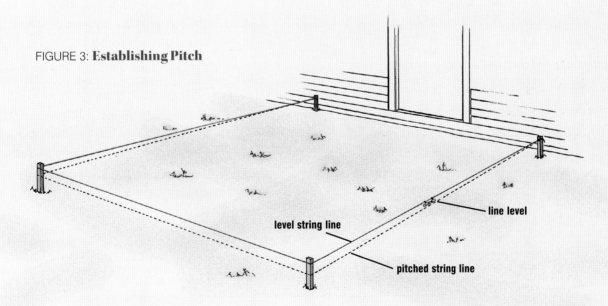

level string line

line level

pitched string line

■ Building Forms for a Concrete Base

If your soil trench isn't stable enough to contain the concrete, you'll have to build forms (see figure 4). The formwork for a concrete base is similar to that for footings, so you may want to review the instructions on page 65. Keep in mind that, in this case, you want the surface of the base (which will be level with the top of the form boards) to be just far enough below ground level to accommodate the mortar bed and all but the top inch of the stones. The forms should be strong enough to contain the concrete. Usually forms are made of two-bys and stakes, but if you have a lot of curves in your design, you can use a saw to rip strips of plywood and attach that to the stakes instead to create your forms. (If you hose down the plywood, it will bend more readily.) I find it easiest to set the stakes first, use a string line and line level to level them up, and then attach the plywood to them.

■ Adding Gravel and Wire Mesh

Add gravel to the excavation, spreading it evenly and tamping it down after every 1-inch layer. You want the gravel to stop about $\frac{1}{2}$ inch below the bottom of the form boards. Brush any type of oil on the interior of the boards so they won't stick to the concrete base. Before you pour the concrete, it's a good idea to add heavy-gauge wire mesh that will prevent the concrete pad from separating if it ever cracks. Set the wire mesh on stones or bricks to raise it above the gravel so it will be approximately in the center of the poured base (see figure 5).

FIGURE 4: **Formwork for a Concrete Base**

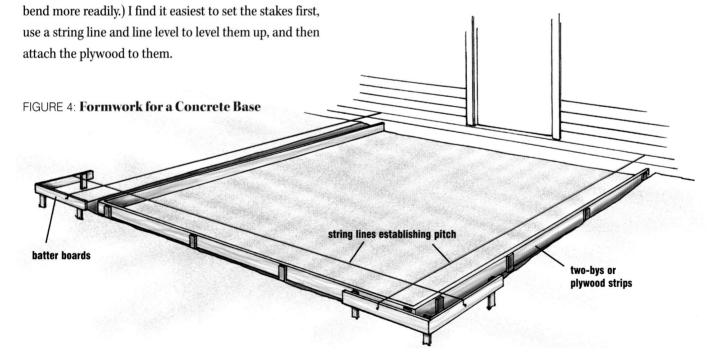

batter boards

string lines establishing pitch

two-bys or
plywood strips

■ Pouring Concrete

Review the information on page 66 about buying and mixing concrete. Remember to have gloves, safety glasses, all your materials and tools, help available, and the site cleared and clean before you start mixing and pouring the concrete.

Pour the concrete into your walkway or patio form, dumping it in mounds that reach just $\frac{1}{2}$ inch above the top of the form boards. You want to pour each mound up against the previous one to avoid separate piles. Use a rake or shovel to spread the concrete around, and slice it with a hoe or shovel to remove any air pockets.

Once you've poured 4 feet of the concrete, stretch a 2x4 that's about a foot longer than the formwork is wide along the top to screed (level off) the concrete (refer to figure 5 again). Shake the 2x4 as you go to help the concrete settle (it will also help remove air pockets). If you have places without enough concrete, add more and screed again. Trowel the concrete off on top, but don't worry too much about getting it smooth. A little texture will actually help the stonework bond to the base. Let the concrete dry for at least one day before laying stone. Remove the form boards after the concrete cures.

FIGURE 5: **Screeding Concrete**

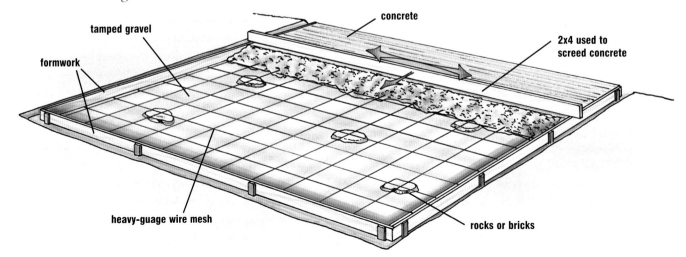

Laying Concrete Block

Most of the mortared stonework I do calls for veneering rather than building with solid stone. Veneered stonework is simply a type of facade used to cover the surface of a block or wood-frame structure. Veneering requires less stone, mortar, and labor than building solid-stone structures, so it saves time and money.

When veneering, concrete block (see figure 6) is often used as the backing wall, or core, to which the stones are then adhered. Using this wall as the backing for your stonework gives you a gauge from which to measure the veneer stones and eliminates the need for stone backfill. This will also ensure that the face of your stonework is plumb.

If your project is complicated—a tall retaining wall, for instance—hire a block mason to build the block structure, and then you can add the veneer. But for simpler projects, you can lay the block yourself. Because the blocks are large and uniform in size and shape, most do-it-yourselfers find block work fairly quick and easy. Here are the basics of using concrete block for mortared stone projects.

Types of Blocks

Blocks you buy today will typically have a nominal measurement of 8 x 8 x 16 inches. If you get out a ruler, you'll see they're actually $7\frac{5}{8}$ x $7\frac{5}{8}$ x $15\frac{5}{8}$-inches; this allows for a $\frac{3}{8}$-inch mortar joint. Most of them have two holes, or cells. You can also buy halves that are half the size of regular blocks; these come in handy when laying column cores. Blocks are usually rectangular in shape. (You can buy square blocks, but these usually come in sizes so large that they're impractical for use as column cores.) For walls, standard 8 x 8 x 16-inch blocks work best. For columns, halves are better.

Estimating the Amount of Block Needed

To figure out the number of blocks you'll need for a project, use their nominal size rather than their actual dimensions. To estimate the amount of block needed for a wall, first divide the wall's length (in inches) by one block's length (usually 16 inches), and that will tell you how many blocks you need for each course. Next, divide the wall's height (in inches) by one block's height (usually 8 inches); this will tell you the number of courses of block you'll need. Multiply the number of blocks needed for the wall's length by the number needed for the wall's height, and you'll have the total number of blocks needed. (Add in extras for breakage.) As you can see, your project will be simplest if you design its dimensions to be a multiple of the concrete block's dimensions.

Mortar for Concrete Blocks

Mortar for block laying should be similar in texture to stick-on mortar. Use a 1 to 2 ratio of type S cement to sand, or $\frac{1}{2}$ bag of type S to 9 shovels of sand. Make it somewhat soupy, like stick-on mortar (see page 45), but stiff enough to hold on to the blocks.

Laying Block for a Wall

Begin by excavating and constructing your wall's footing, following the directions provided earlier in this chapter.

■ Laying the First Course

Locate the ends of your proposed wall on the clean footing. Snap a chalk line on the footing to mark the front edge of your wall. Use a trowel to spread two rows of block mortar 8 inches apart on the footing. Set one end block in place on the mortar, aligning its front with the chalk line. Use the handle of your hammer to lightly tap it into place. Check for level across both the length and the width of the block's top. Make any adjustments needed by tapping lightly with the handle of the hammer again. Check that the top of the block is exactly 8 inches from the surface of the footing. If it's too high, tap it down gently with the hammer handle. If it's too low, remove the block, add mortar to the bed, and then reset the block.

Before you set the next block, apply mortar to, or "butter," the end that will butt against the first block. To do so, stand the block on end, put a little mortar on your trowel, and then scrape it on the edges of the block, as if you're cleaning off the trowel (see figure 6). Set this block against the first block, making sure the joint spacing is about $3/8$ inch. Butter and set another block, and then check the level of all three blocks from side to side and front to back. Use the trowel to remove any excess mortar. Once you've set three blocks, use this same method to set three blocks at the other end of the wall.

FIGURE 6: **Laying Concrete Block**

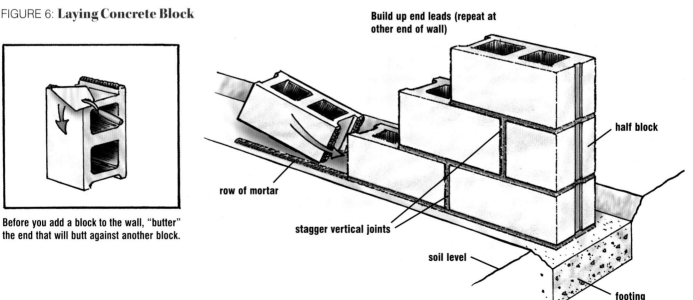

Before you add a block to the wall, "butter" the end that will butt against another block.

Build up end leads (repeat at other end of wall)

half block

row of mortar

stagger vertical joints

soil level

footing

Block steps provide a base for mortared stone, but constructing them is trickier than it looks.

■ Building Up the End Leads

Most blockmasons build up the end leads before laying the rest of the first course. To build up an end lead, lay short courses of blocks on top of these first three blocks until you get to just one block (or one half block and whole block) on the top course (refer to figure 6, page 73, again).

To lay these subsequent courses, spread mortar on the top edges of the previous course, and then set the blocks using the same method that you used for the first course. If you used a full block on the ends of the first course, use a half block on each end in the next course to cross vertical joints. If you can't find half blocks, use a chop saw or the sharp edge of your brick hammer to break a 16-inch block in half. To break a block with a brick hammer, use the sharp edge of the hammer and tap the center of the block all the way around it. Don't hit it too hard or it will break in the wrong spot. Tap it lightly, and work your way around each side in a straight line.

Insert wall ties 16 inches apart between each course of blocks before the mortar dries. Insert one-third of each tie into a horizontal joint.

■ Filling In the Courses

Fill in the remaining blocks, working from each wall end to the middle of the wall. When you get to the final block in a course, butter both its ends and the ends of the blocks on either side of the opening, and slide the block into place. Scrape off excess mortar as you go.

Laying Block for Columns

If you can find them, use square blocks or 12-inch blocks to lay the core for a column. Spread mortar on your footing and set your first block. There's no way to cross joints with these blocks, just mortar and stack them on top of each other, keeping all sides plumb as you work your way up. Level and plumb each block that you set.

Laying Block for Steps

Unless you're a real pro at laying block, I wouldn't suggest attempting to lay the block for steps on your own. The block core for the steps project (in the photo above) was made by a blockmason before I arrived at the site. I knew they were built correctly, saving me a lot of time and frustration. Figuring out the relationship between treads and risers is a tricky business, and getting left with only 1 inch to lay flagstone on your top tread and 12 inches on the bottom is the kind of scenario first-timers often face. Hire a pro to lay block steps, and you can add the stone veneer with confidence.

Metal lath prepares the surface for thin veneer.

Use a hammer and 8-penny nails to attach wall ties to vertical surfaces before thick veneering.

Other Preparations for Vertical Surfaces

Wall ties should be spaced no further than 16 inches apart—closer is fine: you really can't have too many.

Wall Ties

Wall ties are metal fasteners nailed to the wall you are veneering to give the stonework added support. On concrete block, the wall ties should be inserted into the horizontal joints as the block is laid or attached after the block dries. There are several holes in the wall ties for attaching them to the wall. Use one nail or screw in the wall tie hole that's about 2 inches from the end to secure it to the wall.

If you're laying stone on a wood-frame wall, attach roofing felt with a staple gun before you fasten wall ties. Use one 8-penny nail to attach each wall tie to the wood sheathing, preferably driving each nail into a framing stud, which are usually spaced 16 inches apart. Wall ties should be nailed about every 16 inches, both horizontally and vertically.

If you're nailing wall ties to a concrete wall and you can't penetrate the concrete with a nail and hammer, use a load-powered nail gun instead. Check with your local rental store or building supplier for availability.

Attaching Metal Lath to Walls

Metal lath is a sheet of mesh sold in 2½ by 8-foot sections (photo 1). It's attached to wood-sheathed and drywall surfaces and covered with mortar to create a surface to which thin-veneer or manufactured stones can bond. If you're laying stone on a wood-sheathed wall or drywall, use a vapor barrier such as roofing felt between the lath and the wall to prevent the wet mortar from damaging the wall material. Roofing felt is sold in rolls and can be nailed to the wood with roofing tacks or staples. Use at least 1-inch roofing nails to attach lath to the wall around the edge and in the center, and try to hit a stud if possible. Make sure the lath is flat against the wall before nailing to prevent bulges in the surface. Place nails around the edge and in the center of the lath. If you have a relatively large surface area, consider renting an air compressor and nail gun to attach the lath. Use sheet metal screws and a battery-powered drill to attach the lath over the metal faceplates on metal fireplace inserts.

Applying a Scratch Coat

If you're laying manufactured stones or stick-on natural stone on a wood-sheathed wall or drywall, you need to apply a scratch coat of mortar first to give the stones a proper base on which to adhere. The bond will be weak until it cures, which usually takes about 24 hours. The scratch coat mortar recipe is similar to the mortar mix for jointed style (1 part Portland cement, 3 parts sand, and water), but it needs to be soupier, so it spreads over the lath (photo 2). You have your mix right if the trowel slides smoothly across the lath and the mortar sticks to the lath. If the mortar won't trowel smoothly and leaves lumps in the scratch coat, the mortar is too dry. If it runs down and drips instead of sticking, it's too wet. Make adjustments to the mortar by adding water or more sand and cement.

To begin applying a scratch coat, first use tape to outline the area where you'll be laying stone. This will both give you a boundary and it will prevent mortar from staining the wall. Be sure to tape any areas you don't want to get stained, including metal faceplates on fireplaces. Cover the entire area with a vapor barrier and metal lath, following the directions in Attaching Metal Lath to Walls.

Use a stucco trowel to apply a smooth coat of the scratch coat mortar over the lath. Hold your stucco trowel with the handle facing down, and apply a small amount of mortar on the stucco trowel with a brick trowel (refer to photo 2 again). Tilt the stucco trowel toward the wall, starting at the bottom and spread a layer of mortar over the lath (photos 3 and 4). The stucco layer should be about $\frac{1}{2}$ to $\frac{3}{4}$ inch thick. After it dries for 30 minutes to 1 hour, scratch horizontal lines into the surface with a scarifier, or the tip of your trowel, to give the surface a little texture that will help stones stick to the wall (photo 5). The lines should only extend about halfway into the scratch coating. Wait one day before sticking your stones to the wall.

After enough practice, swinging the hammer and hitting the stone in just the right spot will become second nature to you.

Cutting and Shaping Stone

The best way to become efficient at breaking and shaping stone is practice, practice, practice. Working with stone requires a lot of just getting the feel for it. Until you get the knack of precisely where and how hard to hit a stone, it will be a challenge for you to break it in the right spot. But once you do get the hang of it, you'll know exactly where to place that blunt chisel and how hard to strike it to make a perfect cornerstone, and you'll be able to work more quickly and lay more square feet of stone in a given amount of time. All it takes is experience to be able to shape stones just the way you want them.

I recommend taking a few stones out of the pile and practicing shaping them using both ends of your brick hammer, as well as a stone hammer and various chisels. (Just don't waste good stones such as natural cornerstones and straight edges on these practice rounds!) Remember to always wear safety glasses and gloves when breaking, cutting, and shaping stones.

Choosing Stone to Cut

Sandstone and limestone are usually easy to break with a hammer. Dense stone like granite is difficult and usually requires a stone hammer and chisel. If you're building a structure such as a column that requires cutting a lot of corner-stones, avoid dense stone. For thicker stones, larger than 3 inches, you'll need a blunt chisel and a 3- to 4-pound stone hammer. When you need to chisel stone, look for ones that are uniform in color on both the outside and inside. The outer surfaces of some stones, fieldstones in particular, are a different color when you break them open. Then again, sometimes you can incorporate this contrast into your design.

Using a Hammer

A brick hammer (photo 1) has a sharp tip and a blunt tip. The blunt tip is used for knocking larger edges off a stone, and the sharp tip is used for refining jagged edges. For example, if you have a 12-inch-long stone that you want to shorten to 10 inches, use the blunt side to take away about 1 inch at a time. Trust me, stones often don't split the way you want them to the first few times you try this. The best advice I can give on splitting stone with a brick hammer is to take a few stones and see how each end of the hammer works.

Shaping with a Chisel

The blunt chisel is my personal favorite and is probably the most versatile. I use it for all kinds of shaping and fitting techniques: for breaking away large sections along an edge to reduce a stone's dimensions (photo 2), for knocking away large high spots that keep a stone from seating solidly, and for squaring up or otherwise trimming edges so they'll fit properly. I also use it for cutting capstones for a column, hearth, or retaining wall, and to cut cornerstones for columns or wall ends. A blunt chisel is to a stone mason what a wood chisel is to a woodworker; you use it to accurately take off little pieces at a time,

the way a woodworker chisels away wood a few chips at a time. The trick to using chisels is to first visualize how you want the stone to break, and then use the right chisel at the

appropriate angle to make it happen. Hold a blunt chisel at a 45 to 60° angle as you work, striking the chisel sharply as many times as it takes and moving it along the line where you want the stone to break.

A hand-point chisel is the right size and shape for removing a small knot. Just hold the chisel against the side of the knot at a 45 to 60° angle, and strike it hard with a rock hammer. Sometimes the knot will pop right off; in other cases you'll need to chip away at it to remove it all.

To break a stone with a hand-tracer chisel, first place the stone flat on the ground and measure to determine where you need the rock to split (photo 3). Position the chisel at a 90° angle to the seam where you want the stone to break (photo 4), and hit the chisel solidly with your hammer. If the rock doesn't break immediately, move the chisel along the seam, striking it as needed. Then turn the stone over and split it down the same seam from the other side. When you've worked your way around the stone, bridge it across two other stones, and hit it with the blunt end of your stone hammer (photo 5). It should break in half into two corners (photo 6).

Cutting with a Hammer in Hand

Most stonemasons trim or break a small stone by placing it in their hand and then hitting the stone with a hammer. This allows them to position the stone closer to the stonework to see if it fits. Sure, it'll make your hand a little sore at first, but you'll get used to it. Always wear gloves when you do this. To break a stone in half, position the center of the stone in your palm and hit the stone with the blunt end of the hammer. It should break in half (the stone, not your hand). You might have to do this several times before the stone breaks. If it won't break, put it on the ground and hit it with a rock hammer in the center.

To shape the edge of a stone with the sharp end of a brick hammer, hold the rock with the side you're trimming away from your palm, and hit it with the hammer. If the hammer is sharp, the edge of the stone will chip right off. If it's dull, it might not make an even cut. Make sure you hold the rock far enough away so that if you miss, it won't hit your palm. When breaking a stone, flipping it over several times and hitting both sides will give you a more even break.

Cutting Manufactured Stone

Manufactured stone is very brittle and can be difficult to manipulate with a hammer; instead, use a small, electric angle grinder with a 4- to 5-inch masonry blade to cut it. The safest way to do this is to place the stone on a board on the ground and overhang the end you want to cut. Hold the opposite end of the stone down with your foot or your hand as you make the cut. Wear eye and ear protection as well as a dust mask.

Laying Stone

When I lay stone my goal is to make something that's handsome, useful, and enduring. I could say that this involves thinking like an artist and a physicist at the same time, but that sounds unnecessarily intimidating. A lot of laying stone is just common sense and learning from trial and error. The following guidelines will get you started; when you're ready to build, refer to the individual projects for more specific instructions.

> **NOTE:** *With the exception of stick-on stone, never lay more than 4 or 5 feet of a wall on a single day. The wall won't be strong enough to support the weight.*

Laying Out a Trial Course Before You Mortar

It's always safe to lay a trial course to see if the stones will fit, and to see if you'll like the pattern. Once you lay stones in mortar, it's hard to make a change. A trial course will also allow you to pull out a stone and change its shape if necessary. If you're laying a cornerstone for a column, for instance, you should set a trial corner to see if the edge is straight and if it's plumb on the wall. If you don't like it or you can't get it plumb, it will be much easier to pull it off now rather than after it has been tied in with stones and mortar. As you dismantle your trial course, set the stones in order along the sides of the footing so you'll remember which stone goes where.

Laying Stones for Horizontal Structures

The basics of laying stones for horizontal structures (photo 1) can be found in Patios and Walkways, which begins on page 152, and in Steps, which begins on page 164.

Laying Stones for Vertical Veneered Structures

Since most contemporary stonework is veneered rather than solid stone, I'll give you the basics of veneering here. Much of what you'll learn can also be applied to solid-stone construction, and more details are given in the projects that use the solid-stone technique. Veneer, as you'll recall, is a layer of stone covering an understructure of some sort; for vertical structures the base being covered is typically wood sheathing or concrete block. This is the method used for thick veneer (between 6 and 8 inches). For thin veneer, use the stick-on method described on page 92. With thick veneer, you basically lay courses of stone a couple of inches in front of a substructure and then pack mortar behind each course.

Remember, there are two styles of mortared stonework: dry-stack and jointed. (See page 11 for more on the two styles.) When veneering with the jointed style, you leave a small vertical gap between each stone, which you eventually fill with mortar, and you also spread a visible layer of mortar on top of each course of stone before laying the next course. With the dry-stack style, you don't leave vertical gaps between stones, you instead fit stones close together. A very thin layer of mortar is used between each course of stone, but that's scratched out so it's almost invisible. I'll describe how to lay stone in the dry-stack style. Most of this same information will apply if you're using the jointed style; instructions for what you'll need to do differently for that style follow.

■ Keeping Vertical Veneer Plumb

When veneering a wall, it's important to keep the overall face as plumb as possible. Use a level to check the structure you'll be veneering before you lay stone (photo 2). Most concrete block or wood-sheathed walls are built plumb, and that should keep your veneer plumb as you build. If your substructure isn't plumb, you'll need to use a level to plumb the face of the veneer as you work your way up.

■ Setting Cornerstones and Starting the First Course

Always start from the bottom and work your way up. After your wall ties are in place and your footing is clean (photo 3), spread a 2-inch-thick, 3-foot-long layer of mortar at each end of the footing (see page 42 for details on mixing mortar). Start with corners or wall ends first; then proceed to fill in between with other stone sizes and shapes.

Cornerstones have two faces that meet to form a corner. Larger cornerstones make the wall look stronger. Tall cornerstones can equal several courses of stacked stones. Lay a cornerstone in the mortar bed a couple of inches in front of your substructure, and rock it just a bit to get rid of air pockets. Tap it with a rubber mallet to level it. Do the same with another cornerstone at the other end of the structure. After you set the corners, start working your way toward the center by setting enough stones in place next to each cornerstone to cover the mortar beds. See Choosing Stones As You Go for tips on selecting and fitting stones and Pulling Strings for Straight Corners (page 90) for information on keeping corners straight.

With the dry-stack style, it's very important to set your stones as close together as possible so they hide the mortar that will go behind the stones. You may need to chisel the tops and sides of some stones to make them fit together (see Cutting and Shaping Stones on page 78). If you place a stone on the wall and are unhappy with the way it sits or its overall appearance, take it off and make changes before you set it in mortar. If you're laying stones in the horizontal stone pattern (see page 52), which consists of primarily flat, horizontal stones stacked on top of each other, use a level after setting each stone. If all your stones are level, and one is set at an angle, it will stick out like a sore thumb.

Choosing Stones As You Go

Laying stone is a bit like putting together a puzzle with pieces that don't ever fit perfectly. Some stonemasons spend a lot of time searching for just the right stone, and some spend a lot of time cutting and shaping to create that elusive perfect fit. Keep the following pointers in mind when it comes to choosing stones and making them fit.

◆ **Get to know your stone.** Finding the right next stone as you build actually starts back at the sorting stage. As you group your stones according to function (cornerstones, bottom stones, caps, etc.), pay attention to the size, shape, and color of each stone. This will help you remember what you've got when you're trying to fill a particular space. As you can see in figure 7, how you fill a space can vary depending on the stones you have. Eventually, you'll also learn how to create spaces to use the stones you have.

◆ **Reevaluate each stone again as you're laying.** Consider how each surface will work as a top, face, base, or side. Look for right angles and degree of flatness. Assess how this stone will fit with the stones next to it.

◆ **As you lay one course of vertical stone, always think ahead to the next course.** Planning ahead as you place your stones will make laying the next course that much easier. High spots that will get in the way of a future course should be trimmed off before you set the stone.

◆ **Many structures look best with a mix of large and small stones of various colors.** So while you're looking for the right fit, remember, too, to mix things up.

FIGURE 7: **Choosing Stones**

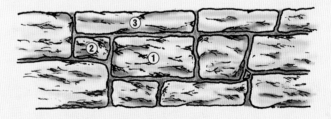

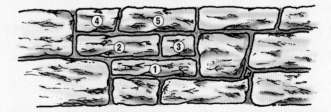

Filling in the Rest of the First Course

Continue to lay stones, working your way from each end toward the center (photo 4), maintaining at least a couple of inches of space between the backs of the stones and the surface against which you're mortaring—this is where you'll pack the mortar (photo 5). Because the stones aren't all uniform in depth, this space will vary from stone to stone. You'll usually lay the entire first course of stones before you pack behind it with mortar, but if your wall is long, lay a few feet within one course before packing mortar behind the stones. Make sure your stones have a sturdy seat before you apply the mortar. If you must trim off a knot or inconsistency to make a stone sit better, this is the time to do it. If a stone doesn't seat properly on the course below, you may need to use a stone chip as a shim or wedge under the front edge to hold the stone in place. Avoid placing stones with their narrow sides down; this could cause the stone to kick out of the wall.

Adding Shiners

If you're integrating shiners—large face stones—into the pattern, place them in the middle of your horizontal courses of stone (photo 6). Shiners can be any thickness and will break up the monotonous pattern of small horizontal stones. Always level to the top edge of shiners so you can cross the vertical joints with the next course of stones. Not only do you want to cross vertical joints with stones in subsequent courses, but you also want to cross horizontal joints. The only way to do this is to lay a stone that's as high as at least two courses of stones.

Packing Mortar behind the Stones

When you're satisfied with the course, trowel mortar between the backs of the stones and the wall. To do so, wear gloves and pack the mortar behind each stone, filling all the voids (photo 7). If the stone moves or shifts out from the wall, hold it in place with one hand while you pack with the other. If you have a large void behind a stone, use small stone chips for fill.

■ Laying Subsequent Courses

When the mortar is packed behind a course of stone, spread a ¼-inch-thick layer of mortar across the tops of the stones and lay another course. Be sure to lay the second course so the stones break the vertical joints of the first course, following the one over two, two over one rule. Alternating short and long cornerstones at wall ends will help ensure that you always cross vertical joints. Once this course is level with your cornerstone, set another corner, alternating the direction of the large face over the narrow end of the previous corner.

■ Scratching Out the Mortar Joints

With the dry-stack style, you scratch out the mortar between the courses of stone so that it doesn't show, leaving the impression that the structure was dry stacked (photo 8). It's important to scratch out the joints (also called "tooling" or "raking") at just the right time. If it's too wet, the mortar will smear and can stain the stone. If it's too dry, it'll be hard to scratch out. Test to see if your mortar is ready for tooling by pressing your thumb into it. When it feels firm but will hold the impression of a thumbprint, it's ready. How long it takes the mortar to get to this point will vary, depending on the temperature, humidity, whether that part of the structure is in direct sun or shade, etc. The safest bet is to go back and check your mortar joints every hour to see if they're ready for tooling.

Once the mortar is ready, take a pointing trowel or small stick and use it to scratch out any visible mortar in the joints. If you've used shims or plugs, make sure they're set deep so they won't fall out when scratching. Use a whiskbroom to remove any mortar on the faces of the stones. (Scratching out jointed-style joints is explained on page 90.)

▌Capping

Many mortared structures (whether veneered or solid stone, dry stack or jointed) require a cap, or a course of finishing stones (photo 9). Traditionally, caps are even in thickness and overhang anywhere from 1 to 3 inches, depending on the size of the surface they're topping. To me, they're as important as the seat on a bench. They must be smooth, somewhat straight, and strong. Strength is a function of making the mortar right and grouting the joints correctly. Smoothness is a function of the type of rock you use and how you manipulate the edges. Capping can be a tedious process, but, when done right, it can also be the most attractive part of a structure.

Before you set the cap, make sure the last course of your wall or other structure is level. This can be accomplished by using a string line as a stopping guide for the last course of stone under the cap (photo 10).

Since capstones will help prevent water from entering the interior of the wall or structure, you want to use fairly wet mortar when setting them, and you want to leave a $\frac{1}{2}$-inch joint between all sides of each stone so you can fill in between with grout. Spread a layer of wet mortar on top of the wall or hearth and use a mallet to tap the stones down. Use a level to make the top smooth. If you tap a stone too low, pick it up and place more mortar underneath it. If you have too much mortar, you'll be better off lifting the capstone and removing a small amount. If you don't have enough large capstones, you can use smaller ones in between larger stones. It's best to let the caps set up for one day before grouting. (See page 159 for more on grouting.)

Jointed-Style Veneering

As I mentioned before, jointed-style veneering doesn't differ all that much from dry-stack style in terms of laying the stone; it's mostly a matter of leaving gaps between the stones and then mortaring these joints.

■ Laying the First Course

Follow the directions for laying a first course for the dry-stack style, but instead of setting stones close together, leave a 1/2- to 1-inch vertical gap between each stone. These gaps, once grouted, provide the visible joints that distinguish this style. Your joints don't have to be exactly 1/2 or 1 inch, but uniform joints are the key to an attractive finished wall.

■ Packing the Joints

After you have a course of jointed-style stones set with mortar packed behind it, you need to pack the gaps between the stones. To do so, take a handful of mortar and, using a pointing trowel, pack the mortar between the stones until the mortar is flush with the face of the stones. To get mortar into the joint, first load it onto your trowel, and then push the mortar into the joint with a quick downward motion (photo 11). This can be a little tricky; an alternative method is to use a trowel to work the mortar down into the spaces between the stones. Load a little onto the trowel near the tip, and smear it into the space between the stones, getting enough mortar in to ensure a good bond. Make sure the joints

are packed solid—the best way to tell is by pushing your finger into the joints. If your finger breaks the surface, you need to repack the weak spots.

■ Mortaring between Jointed-Style Courses

After you've set your first course of stones, packed mortar behind it, and packed the joints, spread a 1-inch layer of mortar across the top of the course. With jointed-style stonework, these horizontal joints will show. Place your next course of stones on top, leaving a 1-inch vertical gap between each stone. Take a hammer or rubber mallet and gently tap each stone about 1/2 inch into the mortar to leave you with a 1/2-inch horizontal joint. If your joint ends up a little larger or smaller, don't worry about it. If it's significantly more or less than that, adjust with the hammer or mallet or take the stone off the wall and adjust the mortar bed.

Scratching Out Jointed-Style Joints

Since the exposed joints are such a visible part of the finished appearance of this style, take the time to scratch out correctly. Make sure the mortar doesn't get too hard. On a hot day, you'll need to check it frequently. Take a pointing trowel or a small dowel and scratch the mortar back until it's recessed about $\frac{1}{2}$ to 1 inch behind the edges of the stones (photos 12 and 13). (See page 56 for various joint styles.) If the mortar falls out of the joint, repack the gaps with fresh mortar. After you've scratched out, take a whiskbroom and brush away the excess, leaving a nice uniform joint around the edges of the stone. If you let the mortar get too hard, you may need to use a wire brush to scratch it out.

Laying Stone for Solid-Stone Structures

Solid-stone construction (photo 14), rather than veneer, is still used sometimes to build garden walls, columns, fire pits, and the supports for benches. You can use either the dry-stack or jointed style for solid stone projects. Laying stones for solid-stone construction really doesn't differ a whole lot from veneering. The main difference is that instead of laying stones against a concrete block or wood substructure, you're creating the structure itself, usually by stacking walls of stone around a rubble and mortar interior. See the individual project instructions for details on this construction method.

Pulling Strings for Straight Corners

When you're building corners on fireplaces, columns, wall ends, or any kind of stonework where two sides meet to form an angle, you need to make your vertical line as straight and plumb as possible. (If you're trying to achieve a rustic pattern with jagged faces, don't bother with corner strings, let your eyes be the judge.)

There are two ways to get a corner straight: pull a straight line from the top to the bottom with nylon string, or use a level to plumb each cornerstone as you set it. Pulling strings is a bit time consuming, so you can use a level if you're only setting a few cornerstones. However, if

Using a plumb bob to pull strings ensures neat, straight corners.

FIGURE 8: **Pulling Strings for Straight Corners**

your corner is more than 4 feet tall, I'd go ahead and pull strings (see figure 8); it will save you a lot of time in the long run. To pull strings, you'll need masonry or 8-penny nails, a hammer, nylon string, a framing square, a plumb bob with string, and 2x4s.

The first thing you need to do is determine where to tie the string. To do so, first calculate the depth your veneer will be. Let's say 6 inches for the sake of example. Then use a framing square to find the point that's 6 inches from both sides of the wall, and mark this spot on the ceiling. Drive a nail into the spot, and drop a plumb bob to the floor. Drive a nail into the spot on the floor, and tie a string tight between the two nails. This will give you a line to lay your corner by. Keep the corner about ⅛ inch from the string as you lay each course.

If you don't have something to attach the nails to at the top, as with most columns or chimneys, you'll have to create a place to attach the top of the string. Nail a piece of plywood that's the exact dimension of your finished column to the top of your block core. Set a nail in each corner and pull strings to the ground.

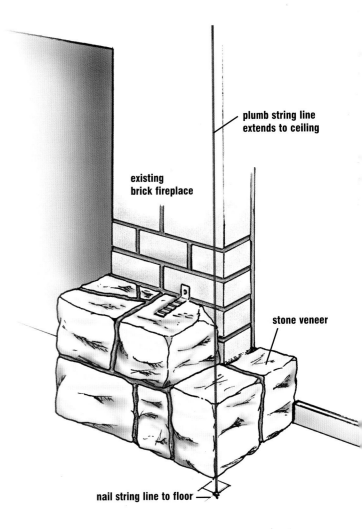

plumb string line extends to ceiling

existing brick fireplace

stone veneer

nail string line to floor

Stick-On Technique for Thin Veneer and Manufactured Stone

Thin veneer consists of thin stones (less than 2 inches) that are not supported by the stones beneath them as thick-veneer stones are; they are instead stuck to a surface with an especially sticky type of mortar applied to the back of each stone. This technique is called the stick-on technique, and thin veneer is often referred to as stick-on stonework. This is the technique used to apply both thin natural stone and manufactured stone.

Thin-veneer usually requires less structural support than thick-veneers, and doesn't require a footing on which to stack the stone; also, the stones are a bit easier to work with. You still need plenty of workspace, but the surface preparation is different. If you're laying on a block wall, no preparation is necessary. If you're laying to a wood-sheathed wall, you'll need to attach a moisture barrier, a layer of metal lath and apply a scratch coat; instructions for both of these processes can be found on page 72. Wait one day between applying the scratch coat and sticking your stones to the wall.

Sticking the Stones to the Wall

This can be the dirty part of the job if you haven't used wet mortar before. Known as "buttering" by most stonemasons who use this style, this process involves spreading mortar on the back of a stone and sticking it to the block wall or a scratch coat on a wall. The process is the same for both thin natural and manufactured stone. The recipe for stick-on mortar can be found on page 41. Spread a ½- to ¾-inch layer of this mortar evenly on the back of a stone. Don't spread too much mortar on the stones, or it will overflow onto adjacent stones. Press the stone against the wall until some of the mortar comes from behind the edges. You might have to hold the stone in place for a few seconds until it sets. If it falls, use fresh mortar to reset it.

Manufactured Stone

Manufactured stone is a cost-effective alternative to natural stone. It's also much lighter, making it easier to work with. If you're considering an interior project inside your home, manufactured stone may be your only option if you don't have a foundation or a solid structure to support the weight of real stone. (If you're ever unsure if your home will support any type of stonework, contact a professional contractor or engineer.)

Manufactured stone can be used in place of real stone for any project. If you're laying in the dry-stack style, start from the bottom as you would with real stone. Manufactured stone has pre-formed corners, so start with the corners and fill in between with smaller, horizontal stones. Sprinkle shiners into the pattern as you feel necessary. If you're using the jointed style with manufactured stone, start from the top so that if stones fall off the wall—a common occurrence if the temperature is too hot or too cold—there won't be stones below they can disturb.

Site Cleanup

At the end of your project, you'll find that you have accumulated a lot of waste, including cement bags, a large pile of rock chips, and a scattered pile of sand. This is when a pickup truck will come in handy. Don't be overwhelmed; this mess is fairly easy to clean up, and when you do, your project will be complete and will take on a different look without all the distractions.

Start by cleaning up around the stonework. Use a blower or a broom to remove all the dust and excess mortar from between the stones. The cement that fell to the ground while you were laying the stones will be hard to loosen with a shovel, so use a mattock to separate it from the ground and a sledgehammer to break it into small pieces. If you have a place in your landscape for debris, such as a hole that needs fill dirt, put the mortar and stone chips there. Another good place is behind a retaining wall or at the bottom of a planter. Otherwise, use a wheelbarrow or 5-gallon buckets to dump debris into the back of your truck. Your local landfill will accept this type of waste, but your local trash collector probably won't.

If you have any culled stone, or leftovers that you didn't use, perhaps they can be saved for a future project. If not, check with a local landscaper to see if they might be interested in buying the stone from you. I don't throw away any leftover stone, since most of it is so expensive. If you can't resell the stones, hang on to

them; I can assure you that your newfound propensity for stonework is sure to create a need for these stones sooner or later. If you can't use the leftover sand in your landscape, add it to the stone chips and mortar debris for disposal. If you used a mortar mixer, you'll find a pile of hard, dry mortar on the ground where you rinsed it after each batch. Separate it from the ground with a mattock and dispose of it, too. If you have a lot of empty cement bags left over after the job, stuff them into the bag that was used to cover the pallet of cement. This bag will also accommodate any other trash that's around the site. Heavy-duty garbage bags also come in handy.

The more help you have for cleanup, the better. I usually set aside at least half of a day to clean up a job, depending on how large it is. Don't forget to return any equipment you might have rented. If you're doing more than one project, you might want to wait until you finish all of them before you begin to clean up.

Projects

You've got the hang of swinging the hammer, angling a chisel, building a footing, and setting the stones to create strong, long-lasting structures. You've mastered the basics, now you're ready to tackle some projects.

So where do you start? Look around your yard or even inside your home and I'll bet you'll find all sorts of places that can be enhanced with stone. Consider erecting a column or two to mark your driveway entrance or giving that old patio slab out back a new look. The projects that follow cover both vertical and horizontal mortared stonework and range from a simple bench to a more-challenging veneer for a fireplace. You can follow the instructions closely or use them as a stepping-off point for whatever mortared-stone projects you have in mind. If you're new to stonework, you probably want to start small and simple and then go from there, but the important thing is to start.

Benches

Add a stone bench to your yard and you'll not only gain a place to sit and enjoy nature, you'll also be creating a piece of sculpture to accent your landscape. Stone benches combine form and function and are relatively easy to construct. If built properly, a stone bench will last forever.

These outdoor seats can vary from a simple smooth slab bridging two vertical stones to a more elaborate retaining wall with a stone backrest. In this chapter, I'll show you how to build a bench that uses a large slab for the seat and two small columns of stones for leg supports. Build the bench in the shade of a tree and you'll have a nice place to rest after a long day of gardening.

A one-piece stone cap will look good in just about any location. Find a stone that's relatively smooth for the seat. Keep in mind, though, that the size of your bench can determine whether or not this is a do-it-yourself job. A large slab will be heavy and awkward to lift by yourself. Keep your bench height between 16 and 20 inches.

A Mortared Stone Bench

Tools and Materials

In addition to the Basic Tool List on page 16, you'll need a friend to help lift the slab, and possibly a wheelbarrow to move the slab to the site.

Mortar Recipe

Please refer to the Mortar Mix for Jointed Style recipe on page 41 if you're building the bench supports with jointed-style mortar joints. Refer to the Mortar Mix for Dry-Stack Style recipe on the same page if you're building the bench supports using the dry-stack style.

Choosing Your Stone

The most challenging aspect of building a bench is finding a slab to be used as the seat. Large pieces of sandstone, granite, creek stone, or any stone of medium density usually aren't hard to come by. Most suppliers set such slabs aside; check with your local stone supplier to see if they have one available. Bench seats can be any shape as long as they are at least 3 inches thick, even thicker is better. Thick stones will not crack over time and will help the bench look solid. Two people can usually lift 3- to 5-inch-thick stones, but anything thicker might require more people. Make sure the bottom of the slab you choose is fairly parallel with the top; this will give the bench a symmetrical look and make it easier to level the seat on the two legs.

The stones for the legs (which are two small columns) should be small, good-stacking stones. Make sure you have an abundance of cornerstones since each leg will have four corners. I used granite for this bench, but you might want to use medium-density stone, such as sandstone, because whenever you create small columns, you have to break a lot of stones.

Getting Ready

The first step to building your stone bench doesn't require any building at all. Instead, just relax. Head out into your yard or garden and mosey around until you find a spot that would make a nice place to sit a spell. This might be smack in the middle of a well-planted garden or off in the corner in some quiet, secluded niche. Sites with water features or views are perfect locations for outdoor seating. Just remember to choose a spot that will draw your attention throughout the entire year. Take your time with this part of the project. The bench you'll be building is not something you'll be picking up and moving around!

Measuring for the Footings

You'll need footings beneath the bench's leg supports. Before you know what size and how far apart to make these footings, you need to know what size and how far apart your bench's column-style leg supports will be. This will depend on the size and shape of your slab. To determine the best dimensions and placement for your column-style legs, flip your slab over and draw a square to indicate where each column will eventually connect with the bottom of the seat (photos 1–3). The slab I used in this project worked best with 10-inch-square columns spaced 22 inches on their centers.

You want your columns to be spaced so they fully support the seat and allow the seat to overhang the columns on all sides. If the slab you use for a seat has a very regular shape, plan your columns so the seat will overhang each by an even amount on all sides. If your slab is irregularly shaped, like mine, it will overhang the columns by different amounts on different sides, but do make sure it will overhang by at least a few inches on every side.

Measure from the center of one square on the back of the slab to the center of the other (photo 4, previous page), and mark that distance on the ground with marking spray (photo 5). Each mark indicates the center of one footing.

Digging the Footings

Using the marks on the ground, dig two holes below the frost line in your area (photo 6). Check frequently to make sure your footing holes are wide enough and far enough apart (photo 7). (Footing holes should be 8 to 12 inches wider than the columns will be.) Refer to page 124 for more information on digging footings for columns and check with your local building inspector if you're unsure about footing depth requirements. Use a square point shovel to clean out the footing and make it square so it will properly contain the concrete.

Pouring the Footings

For this project, it's easiest to just buy bags of concrete mix, which contain sand, Portland cement, and gravel, instead of bothering with mixing your own concrete. Add a few inches of gravel to the bottom of the holes, and pour the concrete into the holes so that the top of the footing is just below ground level (photo 8). Let the footing dry for at least a day before you begin laying stone, and then clean off the footings before you start building the bench's supports.

Determine Your Bench's Height

Keep several things in mind when you're determining the height of your bench. A traditional bench is usually 16 to 20 inches above the ground. Subtract the thickness of your stone seat from the overall height to determine how tall you need to make the legs. The bond between the bottom of your seat stone and the top of the legs should have a $\frac{1}{2}$- to 1-inch mortar joint, so include that in your calculations. For example, a seat stone that's 4 inches thick would require 11- to 15-inch leg supports above the ground. If the bench seat is uneven in thickness, you'll have to build one of the legs higher to adjust for the difference.

Building the Column-Style Legs

Since each support is essentially just a small column, you can refer to the column project on page 122 for instructions. The only difference will be that if your legs are not very wide, you'll probably only have enough room to set two cornerstones without any stones in between.

It's a good idea to use the jointed style if your legs are small, so the stones will be bound by mortar. If you have enough room to fill in the center of the columns, you can use the dry-stack style, but the stones need something to bond with. Start with the corners and work your way up the column, rotating corners and crossing as many joints as you can. Use your level to plumb the corners, and check frequently to make sure you maintain a consistent width (photos 9–11).

Use your hand to pack mortar behind each stone after you set it (photos 12 and 13). If you're using the jointed style, leave a ½- to 1-inch mortar joint between each stone and pack mortar around each course with your hand or a tuck pointer before you set the subsequent course (photo 14).

It's usually easiest to build the columns one at a time (photo 15). Before you set the last course of your last support, make sure the columns are level (photo 16). Scratch out the joints (photo 17) after you finish each column, or sooner if necessary. Sweep away the excess mortar. Wait at least one day for the mortar to dry before setting the seat.

Setting the Seat

As soon as the mortar dries, you're ready to set the seat. Spread a 1-inch layer of mortar on top of each column (photo 18). Using two people, place the seat on the mortar bed, making sure it's centered and positioned correctly (photo 19). Place a 4-foot level on top of the bench seat and use a rubber mallet to tap the seat into place, using the center bubble on the level as a gauge. When the seat is set, wait a few minutes, and then scratch away the mortar joint under the seat just slightly. Wait at least two days before sitting on your bench.

Retaining Walls

Mortared stone retaining walls serve the practical purpose of holding a mound or bank of soil in place and turning eroding slopes and steep, uneven terrain into usable yard and garden space. At the same time, they add immeasurable charm to your outdoor setting as they provide natural-looking definition for terraced lawns or create romantic rock edges for planting beds and patios. On flat sites, stone retaining walls can help enliven a landscape by containing imported soil to create raised beds and borders.

In this chapter, I show you how to build a dry-stack-style, solid-stone retaining wall with horizontal fieldstones on a moderately sloping site. If you prefer, you can use the jointed style instead when you build your retaining wall. Just follow the instructions for that style, which can be found throughout the Basics chapter.

This project teaches you the principles and fundamental techniques you need to customize a retaining wall for any similar setting. If you need to retain a bank much taller than 3 feet, consult an expert before proceeding.

Solid-Stone Retaining Wall

Tools and Materials

In addition to the Basic Tool List on page 16, you'll need marking spray or a garden hose to mark the border, 2-inch-diameter PVC pipe, and a handsaw to cut the pipe.

Mortar Recipe

Refer to the recipe for Mortar Mix for Dry-Stack Style on page 41 for dry-stack stonework or the Mortar Mix for Jointed-Style recipe on that same page for jointed stonework.

Choosing Your Stone

Because your retaining wall will be backed with dirt, only the face of the wall and the capstones will be visible. You'll need attractive stone for these parts, plus a supply of backfill. Culled stone, scrap block, brick, or any type of stone will make sufficient backfill; I prefer riprap or inexpensive quarried stone.

For a solid-stone retaining wall, like the one in the photo, I like to use stones that are large enough to extend into the wall. This makes the structure stronger, and it means I don't need to do as much backfill work. Other than that, finding the right type of stone is really a matter of just finding one that appeals to you.

With a veneered retaining wall, the type of stone you use doesn't really matter either; although, as with any type of stonework, sandstone and limestone are easy to shape with a hammer. I'd steer away from most types of granite since they're so hard to shape. If your veneer is 6 inches, use stones around 3 to 4 inches thick so you have room for mortaring them in and you don't have to trim as much. For a dry-stack style, stones with a flat top and bottom work well because they'll sit comfortably on top of each other. I like to place large stones at the wall's bottom to help the wall look anchored and stronger, but, structurally, that's not really important.

Choose capstones for your wall carefully, since they can have a strong effect on the wall's appearance. You'll usually need capstones that are 3 to 4 inches thick. Capstones that are the exact depth of the top of your wall will give it a more formal appearance.

Getting Ready

The height and angle of the bank you're retaining will determine the height of your wall. Usually, the steeper the slope, the higher the wall must be. Walls above 3 feet typically require the expertise of an experienced stonemason or even an engineer, and may be subject to local building codes and permits. Lower walls, like the one I show you how to build here, are perfect for containing moderate slopes and providing a spot to plant flowers or small shrubs.

FIGURE 1: **Retaining Wall**

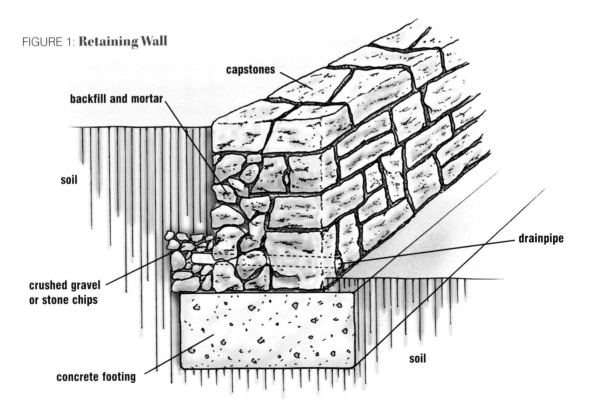

capstones

backfill and mortar

soil

crushed gravel or stone chips

concrete footing

drainpipe

soil

■ Excavating the Bank

For most low walls, you'll be able to excavate the soil bank with a mattock, a shovel, and a little physical labor. For retaining walls longer than 20 feet, or walls with soil banks over 3 feet high, you should consider renting a piece of equipment such as a track hoe or a front-end loader. If you dig out the bank to exactly the same width as the finished wall will be, it'll be easy to backfill the wall, and it will prevent your mortar from falling down in the space between the bank and the back of the wall. Save the soil you remove, since you may need it later to dress out the area behind your finished wall. Save any stones you encounter when excavating the bank to use as backfill.

Digging and Pouring the Footing

Mark the boundary where you want your wall with marking spray (photo 1). Loosen the soil along the marked line with a mattock (photo 2), and then use a shovel to dig a trench for your footing (photo 3).

A concrete footing is the foundation on which your retaining wall will sit. Without a footing, frost heave or settling is likely to impair the integrity of your wall. Footings are absolutely necessary in locations where the ground freezes. Building codes vary, so check with your local building inspector if you're unsure about requirements for your area. More detailed instructions for building footings can be found on page 64, but here are a few pointers for footings for retaining walls:

◆ The footing for a retaining wall 2 feet or taller should be 8 inches deep (the bottom of which should be 12 inches below the soil, or below the frost line in your area) and at least 8 inches wider than the thickness of your wall. For a shorter retaining wall, you can make your footing only 4 inches deep, but I still recommend putting it below the frost line.

◆ The soil you dig out to create the trench for your footing makes perfect topsoil for planting behind your wall.

◆ If you're pouring a small footing, consider mixing your own concrete. For small projects, such as this one, you can also save time and money by mixing premixed concrete or by mixing a few batches of a wet mixture of the standard mortar mix and pouring it into the footing. It's essentially the same mix as concrete mix, only it doesn't have gravel. Make the mixture soupy enough to be poured into the footing and spread with a trowel.

Preparing a Footing on a Slope

If your footing is on an incline, you might need to step up the trench so that the concrete doesn't run to the bottom of the slope. The slope on the upper right side of the trench we dug for this wall was steep enough that I wanted to break it up with some simple steps, to ease the flow of the cement I'd be adding. Rather than build a wooden form to keep the cement from flowing over the steps, I used a stone at each step. This essentially made each stone part of the footing, giving me a solid masonry foundation on which to build the retaining wall.

Laying the Base Course

Before you start laying stone, pound some stakes into the ground and attach a string level where the top of your wall will be to serve as a guide as you work. Spread a 1-inch layer of mortar, and begin by setting the front cornerstone at one end of the wall (photo 4). If you have a dip in the footing, make up for it by making the mortar bed thicker in the low spot.

Set the first course of stones for the face of the wall (photo 5), checking after every few stones to make sure your work is level. The retaining wall I built for this project is in the dry-stack style using mostly medium-size fieldstones. It's very important to keep each stone level when you're laying horizontal stones. If you're using the dry-stack style, keep the joints as tight as possible to give it a cleaner look. With the jointed style, keep all vertical and horizontal joints to a minimum, $\frac{1}{2}$ to 1 inch wide.

When you get to the wall end, consider turning the wall into the bank so that the retained soil doesn't wash out. In this project, I turned one corner in about 90° and

left the other straight. Use your best judgment according to the landscape and the overall shape of your wall. Retaining walls on very slight slopes probably don't need to turn in, but walls on dramatic slopes certainly do.

Lay the back edge of your backfill stones 16 to 18 inches from the face of the wall, placed so the straight edges of the stones are against the back of the trench (photo 6). Then use stone chips and rubble to fill the void between the two rows of your first course of stone. Use your hand to pack mortar tightly between the stones in the face of the wall and the backfill stones, filling in all cracks and voids (photo 7).

Adding the Remaining Courses

Since a short retaining wall like this has only a few courses of stone, pay special attention to making each course level. One stone that's not level will be very obvious and will throw the entire pattern off, making it look sloppy and unbalanced. The easiest way to make each stone level with the next is to set a stone, place your level on it and also over the empty space beside it, and measure the distance from your previous course to the bottom of your level (photo 8). That distance is how thick you need your next stone to be. Make sure you cross both vertical and horizontal joints. To cross horizontal joints, stack two stones beside one tall one to break a horizontal running bond (photo 9). Keep this in mind as you're building the entire wall, especially the corners. If you're laying stone in the hot sun, scratch the joints every 3 to 4 hours with a tuck pointer (photo 10).

A dry-laid retaining wall needs batter (a 5 to 10° difference between the bottom of the wall and the top) because it has no mortar to keep it from leaning forward over time. A properly drained mortared retaining wall that's no taller than 5 or 6 feet doesn't need batter because if you build it thick and solid enough, it will be strong enough to retain whatever pressure is exerted on it.

Adding Wall Drains

Retaining walls are subject to pressure created by wet soil behind them. If you plan for your wall to be 3 feet tall or higher, you'll need to install wall drains. You can use a handsaw to cut your drains out of 2-inch-diameter PVC pipe or use any other heavy-duty conduit. Make them 2 to 4 inches longer than the thickness of your wall. They should be set at 6- to 8-foot intervals along the length of the wall, 4 to 6 inches above the finished level of the soil on the front face of the wall. I usually cut all my drains before I begin constructing a wall and space them out on the ground where they'll be located, so I won't forget to put them in.

Integrate your drains into your wall between stones and secure them with mortar. Place backfill of small stone chips or gravel behind the wall drains before backfilling with dirt. A 5-gallon bucket of rubble or gravel will be sufficient behind each pipe. Set the drains about $\frac{1}{2}$ to 1 inch inside the face of the wall so they won't be exposed (photo 11). Lay the pipe between two stones so you can bridge the gap with a stone and not crush the pipe. Continue building the wall, mortaring over the pipe just as if it were a stone (photo 12).

Setting the Capstones

If all of your capstones are uniform in thickness, the last course of stones before the cap needs to be level (photos 13 and 14). If it isn't, you might have to use shims under the capstones or use thicker capstones. Refer to page 88 for more information on capping walls.

Wait one day before backfilling the wall with soil. If you're going to use your retaining wall as a planter, you'll probably need to backfill with topsoil rather than fill dirt.

Freestanding Walls

Hundreds of years ago, freestanding walls made of stacked stone enclosed property boundaries, pastures, and gardens. The walls kept out unwanted guests, defined borders, and made use of the very objects that cluttered the soil. Today, freestanding walls can serve many of the same purposes, but they also are appreciated simply as objects of beauty. Whether built with fluid curves and smooth caps or solid, straight lines, freestanding walls can enhance any landscape.

More durable than any type of fence or hedge, a properly built mortared freestanding wall will provide a strong, solid border for your yard. Smaller walls make perfect garden structures, while taller walls can be used to provide privacy and even protection. I've seen a tall freestanding stone wall used as a fence to prevent deer from feeding on expensive plants.

In this chapter, I teach you to build a solid-stone wall in the jointed style. You can, if you choose, build a solid-stone wall using the dry-stack style instead. In the sidebar on page 121, I'll give you information about veneering a concrete block wall.

Building a Freestanding Solid-Stone Wall

Tools and Materials

In addition to the Basic Tool List (page 16), you'll need the following: stakes and nylon string for a string line, and—if the soil where you'll build the footing has roots embedded in it—an axe or a handsaw. Mixing mortar by hand for a long wall can be hard work, so you might want to consider renting a mortar mixer if you don't own one.

Mortar Recipe

Refer to the recipe for Mortar Mix for Dry-Stack Style on page 41 for dry-stack stonework or the Mortar Mix for Jointed-Style recipe on that same page for jointed stonework.

Choosing Your Stone

Except for the bottom, all sides of a freestanding wall are visible, so you'll need an abundance of attractive stone plus a supply of backfill for the wall's center (see figure 1, page 117). Culled stone, scrap block, brick, or any type of stone will make sufficient backfill—I prefer riprap, or inexpensive quarried stone. Since the top of the wall is the most visible portion, pay close attention to choosing capstones. If you want to use the same type of stone for the wall and cap, set the capstones aside before building the wall so they'll be available to you later.

There are two ways to cap a freestanding wall. One way is to make the last course of your wall level and lay a cantilevered cap. The thickness of the stones should be consistent and the top should be somewhat smooth and flat, especially if you'll be sitting on the wall. Make sure the stones for this cap are all the same width so they'll create smooth, formal, parallel lines down both sides of the wall's top. Use capstones that are proportional to the other stones in your wall: 4- to 6-inch capstones will look awkward and out of place on a wall built from 2- to 3-inch stones.

The other way to cap a wall (the method I used for the wall in this project) is to pull a string line and lay the last course so its top is level at the string line. Each stone in this last course will need to have a top that's smooth and flat (it doesn't matter how thick the stones are as long as they all come out level at the top). Since the vertical joints will be visible on the cap, make sure they are varied to avoid running joints.

For the jointed-style wall featured in this project, I collected the stones on the property where the wall is located. Good stone was somewhat scarce, so I used anything I could find; fieldstones, capstones, natural corners, and flat stones. I kept most of the faces natural and used stone chips and culls as backfill.

As with any type of stonework, sandstone and limestone are easy to shape with a hammer, while it's best to leave most types of granite and basalt natural since they're so hard to shape. If you're building a veneered freestanding wall and your veneer is 6 inches, you'll want to use stones around 3 to 4 inches deep so you have room for mortaring them in and you won't have to trim as much. For a solid-stone retaining wall, using smaller stones just means you'll need more backfill. This can be a good thing if you're trying to save money because riprap is generally cheaper than most types of building stone. However, I like to use stones that extend deep into the wall. It makes the wall stronger and means less backfill work.

Getting Ready

Before you begin building, clear the worksite of any debris or obstacles so that you have plenty of room to work. Gather materials and supplies, including stone, sand, cement, mortar mixer if you're using one, shovel, water hoses, and your masonry tools.

Digging and Pouring the Footing

Mark the boundary of your wall with marking spray. Loosen the soil along the marked line with a mattock and then use a shovel to dig a trench for your footing. A concrete footing is the foundation on which your wall will sit (refer to figure 1 again). Without a footing, frost heave or settling is likely to impair the integrity of your wall. The wall I built was 18 inches wide, parallel to the side of a concrete pool deck, so I measured 24 inches off the existing concrete to mark the other edge of the concrete footing. The footing for a freestanding wall should be at least 8 inches deep (the bottom of which should be 12 inches below the soil, or below the frost line in your area) and at least 8 inches wider than the thickness of your wall.

Footings are absolutely necessary in locations where the ground freezes. Building codes vary, so check with your local building inspector if you're unsure about requirements for your area. More detailed instructions for building footings can be found on page 64, but here are a few pointers for footings for freestanding walls:

◆ If you're pouring a small footing, consider mixing your own. For small projects, such as this one, you can also save time and money by mixing premixed concrete or mixing a few batches of a wet mixture of the standard mortar mix and pouring it into the footing. It's essentially the same mix as concrete mix, only it doesn't have gravel. Make the mixture soupy enough to be poured into the footing and spread with a trowel.

◆ Pour the concrete or cement into the trench, and use your shovel, rake, or hoe to spread it out. I usually spread it out with a shovel first, since I can shift more cement around if I need to, and finish smoothing with my brick trowel or a stucco trowel.

◆ Let the footing dry for two days before you lay stone. Cover the footing with plastic if it looks like rain is in the immediate forecast.

Laying the Base Course

First, place two stakes in the ground at each end of where the wall will be, and tie a string between them to establish the wall's height. Use a pencil and straight-edge to mark the edges of the wall on the footing so you can have a guide on which to lay your first course. You should have at least 4 inches of footing extending beyond each side of the wall. (Since the wall in the photos abutted a patio, the footing only extended on one side.)

Use your shovel to spread a 1-inch layer of mortar on the footing at one corner (photo 1). Set a cornerstone and use your level to plumb it (photo 2). After you plumb this cornerstone, set the other cornerstone on the same end of the wall (photo 3). Fill in between with smaller stones. Leave a ½- to 1-inch-wide joint between each stone. Rotate cornerstones so you overlap joints and the stonework looks balanced. This means if you use the small end of a stone on the left corner, use the large face of a stone on the right corner.

FIGURE 1: **Freestanding Solid-Stone Wall**

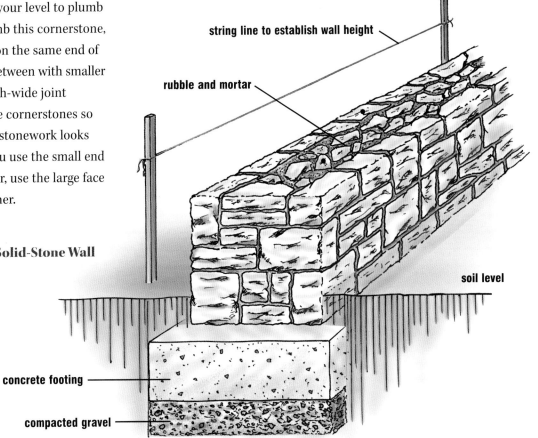

string line to establish wall height

rubble and mortar

soil level

concrete footing

compacted gravel

After you set the corners at one wall end, lay a course of four or five stones along one side of the wall (photo 4). After you lay a few stones, go to the other side and lay a course down that side. Use your tape measure frequently to measure from one side of the wall to the other to make sure the wall's width is consistent (photo 5). Irregular places in the wall will be very obvious when the sun hits it.

After you've set the cornerstones and four or five stones down each side, fill in the center of the stonework with stone chips and cull stone, and fill all voids and cracks with mortar. Use your hand to pack the mortar tightly behind the stones as well as in the joints between each stone. Continue setting the entire base course and the corners at the other end, and fill in with stone chips and rubble (photo 6). Use your hand and tuck pointer to fill in all the remaining cracks (photo 7). After you set the first course and fill in with mortar, begin laying the second course by leveling up to the taller stones with the subsequent courses. Make sure you cross all vertical and horizontal joints whenever possible.

The backfill (culls, chips, and mortar) should be level with the top of each course so that your next stone will sit flat on top of the mortar and not the raised portion of the backfill stone. When you get your backfill between the front and back courses of stone, fill in all the cracks with mortar.

Laying the Remaining Courses

Continue setting the courses of the wall, packing mortar behind each course (photo 8). Cross vertical joints with subsequent courses. Use your hand and tuck pointer to pack mortar in all the joints, voids, and cracks in the wall (photo 9). More detailed directions for both packing and scratching out (photo 10) jointed-styled joints can be found on pages 89 and 90.

Setting the Capstones

Instead of using cantilevered capstones for this wall, I let the top of the last course of stones serve as the cap. I wanted the top surface of this last course of stones somewhat smooth and level to provide a comfortable seat.

When laying this top course, measure the distance between the previous course of stones and the string that marks the height of the wall's cap to make sure you find the right size stones (photo 11). If you can't find the right stone, use a 4-pound hammer and a blunt chisel to shape a stone to fit. Fill in the center of the cap with smooth, flat stones (photo 12). Check for level (photo 13) and measure front to back so the top of the wall stays even and each side is parallel.

Use fairly wet mortar and tap your capstones into place with a rubber mallet, leaving a ½-inch mortar joint between each capstone. If your wall, like mine, is doubling as a bench, this last course of stone will serve as a seat. It will also function aesthetically as the wall's cap, so take the time to place these top stones carefully, and make sure the mortar joints will contribute to the look you want for your wall. Follow the grouting instructions on page 159 to grout between each stone (photos 14–16).

Building a Veneered Freestanding Wall

You might wonder why you even need to bother laying a block wall if a freestanding solid-stone wall is so easy to build. The truth is, anytime you have a block core to veneer, the job is even easier. It reduces the amount of backfill needed, it reduces the amount of mortar needed to fill the center of the wall, it eliminates the need to pull strings for a straight cap, and it keeps the wall plumb and uniform in thickness. A concrete-block core creates a flat surface from which you can measure the distance to the face of each stone, leaving you a uniform, smooth surface.

The footing required for the block core is the same as for a solid-stone wall. You'll build your core with 4-, 6-, or 8-inch-wide concrete blocks. All of these blocks are 8 inches tall and 16 inches long

(once you add ⅜-inch mortar joints), so which block you choose will depend on how thick you want your final wall to be. Remember, you'll be adding a 6- to 8-inch veneer to each side of the block. Refer to the section on laying block on page 72 for more information on block work, or consult a blockmason or stonemason to help construct the block wall.

Make sure your block wall isn't too high. You need to leave about 3 to 4 inches for your stone caps, depending on the type of capstones you're using. For example, if you want the wall to be 3 feet high, you'll need to lay four courses of 8-inch blocks. This will leave you 4 inches to set the capstones. If you're using thin flagstones, leave less space for the cap, and build your veneer a couple of inches above the block

wall on each side to make up for the difference. If 8-inch blocks don't make the wall high enough, use 2- or 4-inch cap blocks to make up the difference. (Check with your local masonry supply store to see if these blocks are available.) Remember as you lay the concrete blocks to set wall ties into the block wall every 16 inches, both vertically and horizontally. If you want to veneer an existing wall that doesn't have wall ties, hammer the wall ties into the mortar joints. Refer to page 83 for more information on veneering block walls.

Columns & Mailboxes

Stone columns can elegantly mark an entrance or drive, serve as graceful supports for a gate, wrap around the base of rustic porch posts, or act as pedestals for pots of flowers beside the steps to your front door. Better yet, building a stone column can be as easy as making the right mortar and having a stack of good cornerstones by your side.

In this chapter, I teach you how to build both a veneered and a solid-stone column. Then, I show you how to adapt the basic column design to incorporate a newspaper cell and a mailbox, resulting in a marker for the end of your front walk or driveway that's as useful as it is attractive. I built the veneered column using the jointed style and the solid-stone one in the dry-stack style, but you can use either style with either approach to create columns that will suit settings ranging from cozy to grand.

Tools and Materials

See the Basic Tool List on page 16.

Mortar Recipe

Refer to the recipe for Mortar Mix for Dry-Stack Style on page 41 for dry-stack stonework or the Mortar Mix for Jointed-Style recipe on that same page for jointed stonework.

Choosing Your Stone

The main building material you need for columns is a good supply of cornerstones—stones that are flat and rectangular in shape, with faces that form roughly 90° angles. Finding perfect 90° corners isn't as important as finding cornerstones that have smooth, flat tops. Because you'll have to do so much hammering and chiseling to shape your cornerstones, it's a good idea to work with stones that are not too dense and therefore easier to break, such as sandstone or limestone. Stone such as granite and creek stone is generally harder to break, and the breaks don't always result in straight corners. You want your column's cornerstones to be 3 to 5 inches thick when stood on their vertical side. This will provide adequate seating when you stand the cornerstones upright. A good way to make two corners out of one large field-stone is to bridge a large stone across two smaller stones and hit it in the center with a sledgehammer. If you hit the large field-stone two or three times in the same line, it should split in a straight line.

In addition to cornerstones, you'll need a supply of stone for filling in between corners, capstones for the top of the column, and—if you're building a solid column—rubble for filling in the core.

Getting Ready

Before you start to build, remove any weeds, shrubs, loose dirt, or debris to create a clean site. This will make digging the footing much easier.

Digging and Pouring the Footing

Detailed instructions for building footings can be found on page 64. Here are some pointers for building footings for columns:

◆ Begin making your column's footing by digging a hole 6 inches wider on each side than the planned width of your column. Check local codes to determine the footing depth for your area. If you're building your column on a slope, dig at least 8 to 12 inches below the lowest part of the grade, so the footing isn't exposed.

◆ If you're building just a small column or two, you can make a few batches of mortar by hand to fill the footings. For a whole series of columns, you might want to hire a concrete truck to deliver the concrete for your footings.

◆ If your column is square, make sure the footing is square. Though footings for columns usually don't have to be perfect, it's best to use a framing square to make sure you're close.

◆ Allow the footing to dry for one day before you start building your column.

Building a Veneered Column

The easiest way to build a column is to start with a concrete block core. As with any type of stonework, the sole purpose of the block core is to make it easier to lay the stone and to keep the column plumb, using the blocks as a gauge from which to measure. You can use either the dry-stack or jointed style to build a veneered column.

Building the Block Core

If the block core for your column isn't already built, lay 12 x 8 x 8-inch blocks or 16-inch flu liners to establish a core. Follow the directions in the Laying Block section that begins on page 72 for instructions on laying block. Let the block dry for one day before setting wall ties and laying the stone.

Veneering the Block Core

Depending on how thick you want the columns, veneer for stone columns should be 6 to 8 inches thick on each side. The easiest way to make sure the corners of your column are straight and plumb is to nail a piece of plywood that's the exact dimension that your stone column will be to the top of the block. Place a nail in each corner and drop plumb lines.

Laying the Courses

To start laying stone, spread a thin layer of mortar on the footing and set a cornerstone. On each side of the column, cornerstones should be rotated to provide a nice balance visually and to overlap joints, preventing running bonds (photos 1 and 2).

NOTE: *If you have wooden columns on your porch and you want to wrap them with stone, nail wall ties and staple roofing felt into the wood and use the technique described for veneering a block column. If the wood isn't straight, use a level to keep the face of the stone portion of the column plumb.*

Once two corners (a large face and an end corner) are set, fill in between with smaller stones (photo 3), packing ½ to ¾ inch of mortar between each one (photo 4). When these stones are level with the tallest corner, move to the adjacent side of the corner and work your way up to the top of the next corner (photo 5). The goal is to build up to the top of each corner each time, so that by the time you reach the top with one corner, the other three will be close behind. Continue this process as you work your way up the column.

Scratching Out the Joints

See pages 87 and 90 for instructions on when and how to scratch out the mortar for the joints (photo 6). Information on various styles of joints can be found on page 56.

Capping the Column

When you reach the top of the column, use stones that are similar in thickness and have flat faces to cap the top of the column (the column in the photos was built around a wooden post for a covered porch). Flagstones work perfectly for this, as long as they match the column in color. Use a mallet to set the capstones in place. I like to overhang the capstones 1 inch over the column. Leave a ½-inch mortar joint between each cap-stone, and use a tuck pointer to pack mortar between each stone. Scratch away the mortar with the edge of the tuck pointer and sweep away the excess.

Building a Solid-Stone Column

Freestanding columns are a perfect way to beautify the entrance to your property or mark your driveway. A taller column, 4 to 7 feet tall, will have enough strength to support a gate.

Laying the First Course

After your footing is poured and has cured for at least one day (see page 64 for instructions for building footings), spread stones around the column site and think about how various arrangements will affect the column's appearance. Spread a thin layer of mortar on one side of the footing and set a good cornerstone. I like to start with a large cornerstone to give the column the appearance of being anchored. Since this is a solid-stone column, you won't have a block core, so make a mental note to yourself to use your level to plumb each cornerstone on both sides.

As with a veneered column, after you lay two cornerstones on one side of the column, fill in between with other stones. Whether you're doing the jointed or the dry-stack style, it's important to lay the top of the stones level with the top of your cornerstones so that you can cross the vertical joint with the next stone.

After you lay a course of stone all the way around the column, fill in the center with stone chips, masonry debris, or broken pieces of block or brick to create a solid core. Pack mortar behind each of the stones by hand and between all voids and cracks inside the column to create a solid core. Use a level to make sure the overall sides of the column are plumb.

Laying Remaining Courses and Capping

After you finish the first course of the column, lay another course until you level up to each of the four corners. This will keep the column consistent and strong as you work your way up. When stones on all sides support each of the four corners, set your second course of corners and fill in between with stones. Just like before, add fill or cull stones in the center after you lay each course. Fill all voids and cracks with mortar so the column is solid. The last course of stone beneath the caps should be as level as possible. Use flat caps with straight edges for capstones. I like to overhang column caps by 1 to 2 inches on each side, depending on the width of the column.

FIGURE 1: **Solid-Stone Column**

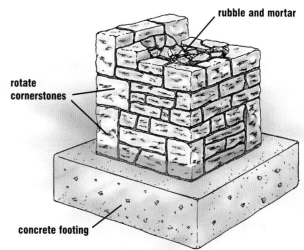

rubble and mortar

rotate cornerstones

concrete footing

Building a Solid-Stone Column with a Mailbox

If you're building a column at the entrance of your driveway, consider spicing it up by adding a mailbox and a newspaper insert. With a solid-stone column, this can be as simple as inserting a metal or wooden mailbox with or without a door and creating a natural void for the newspaper. If you're building a column with a block core, you'll lay the block only as high as the bottom of the newspaper insert or mailbox.

A newspaper box stuck in the ground beside your stone mailbox will take away from the look you're trying to achieve, and it will create an eyesore when it eventually leans and becomes a habitat for mold and climbing weeds. Adding an insert for a newspaper into the column is the best solution. It can be a plastic, metal, or wooden box or cylinder inserted into the column, or, like the one I built, it can consist of just a cell created in the column with stone. Whatever you use to hold newspapers, it's important to design your column ahead of time so you can be sure you have room for the insert, the mailbox, and the column cap and at the same time insure that the mailbox and newspaper insert are at a comfortable height, both for you and the mail carrier.

Adding a Newspaper Box

To add a newspaper box to a column, set the box on top of a level course of stones in the center of the column, and then build around it with stone. Set the opening back 1 inch so that the lip of the insert isn't exposed or sticking out of the column. Treat the opening as if it were a square stone and lay other stones to the top of the newspaper box all the way into the column. Cross the top of these with larger stones so that the weight of the upper half of the column doesn't crush the box.

Creating a Natural Void for Newspapers

If you prefer a natural void instead of a newspaper box, you'll build the column as high as you want the bottom of the cell to be and then create a space within the column that's large enough to shelter a newspaper (see photo 1). Set the stones used to create the cell in mortar. Leave a level place in the center that's 12 to 14 inches wide. Lay the sides of the cell 4 to 6 inches high, making sure both sides are of equal height. Use smooth rocks that won't tear the newspaper.

When both sides are set, continue building the back of the newspaper cell inside the column, perpendicular to the front of the column, enclosing all the spaces to prevent mortar from falling into the cell (photos 2 and 3). Make sure the box is deep enough to allow a newspaper to be enclosed. Fill the rest of the column center with stone chips, masonry debris, or broken pieces of block or brick. Pack mortar behind each of the stones by hand and between all voids and cracks inside the column to create a solid core. After you set the side stones in mortar, cross the top with stones that completely cover the cell, creating a bridge for the interior column to rest on (photos 4 and 5).

Adding the Mailbox

Once your newspaper cell is established, create a level place for the mailbox, setting it on a ½- to 1-inch mortar bed in the center of the column (see photo 6). Remember to leave enough room for the door of the mailbox to open and close. Build the sides up to the top of the mailbox (photos 7 and 8), and then cross them with large, flat stones so that you don't crush the top of it. Finish your column with a nice, even cap (see the project photo on the previous page).

Fire Pits

Turn your yard into a favorite gathering place by adding a stone fire pit. It's a great way to use stones left over from other projects, and if you're building a flagstone patio that's surrounded by a beautifully curved seat wall, a fire pit will be the perfect finishing touch. Even if you don't have a patio, the flickering light and woodsy scent of a fire pit will add ambience to any backyard.

A fire pit can be functional as well. It can provide warmth on cool evenings, keep mosquitoes at bay, and even allow you to cook an outdoor feast. Whether your backyard plans include large formal parties or simple marshmallow-roasts and ghost stories with the kids, a mortared stone fire pit will lure you out under the stars.

A good pit needs a fairly deep well, a hole that allows rainwater to drain, and a smooth collar on which to rest your feet or perhaps set a grill. Fire pits can be built below ground with the top of the ring flush with ground level, or they can be built above ground, like a small, circular freestanding wall. In this chapter, I teach you how to build both kinds.

In some areas, local fire codes specify how and where you can build a fire pit, and, depending on where you live, you may even need to obtain a permit to burn outdoors. Check with your local fire department or other authorities before you begin.

Factor in both convenience and safety when siting your fire pit.

Building a Fire Pit

Tools and Material

See the Basic Tool List on page 16.

Mortar Recipe

Refer to the recipe for Mortar Mix for Dry-Stack Style on page 41 for dry-stack stonework or the Mortar Mix for Jointed-Style recipe on that same page for jointed stonework.

Choosing Your Stone

When you're choosing stones for a fire pit, try to find stones no wider than 12 inches, the typical width of the wall of a fire pit. Don't use stones that are very brittle or soft—a fire pit is a good place to drop wood and throw logs, so the stones must be hard and dense. Set aside any flat, curved-edge stones early on so that you'll have plenty to use for the capstones of your fire pit.

Getting Ready

To get started, you'll first need to determine where you want the fire pit to be located. As a general rule, your fire pit should be sited at least 30 feet from trees, roots, low-hanging branches, or any other combustible material (including wooden structures), but the fire codes in your area may vary, so check local codes before deciding on a location.

Next you'll need to decide how big you want your fire pit to be and whether you want an in-ground or above-ground fire pit. The size of your pit will determine the size of the fires you can build. A smaller diameter ring will allow only short pieces of firewood to be burned and will give off a relatively small amount of heat. A very large ring will allow you to build large fires but will also mean you may need to sit or stand further away from the fire. Most pits I construct have an interior diameter no smaller than 2 to 3 feet with walls that are about 12 inches thick. If you want it to be aboveground, I don't recommend building the walls much higher than 12 to 18 inches.

The pros of an aboveground fire pit are that elevated walls give you a place on which to rest your feet. They also raise the bed of your fire so you can feel the heat more easily and more comfortably fuel the fire with paper and wood. And a closer flame means a closer heat source to cook hot

Smooth capstones can serve multiple functions.

dogs and marshmallows. Another advantage to building a raised fire pit is that there is less excavation involved. The only digging required is a trench for the footing.

■ Building the Footing for an Aboveground Fire Pit

For an aboveground pit, you'll be building a wall very similar to a small freestanding wall, but shaped in a circle. The footing trench for an aboveground fire pit should be dug 8 inches below the ground, and it should be 4 to 6 inches wider on each side than the wall of the fire pit will be (see figure 1). (For the typical 12-inch-wide fire pit wall, this would mean a 20- to 24-inch-wide footing.)

Refer to page 64 for directions on building footings. Pour the footing 4 to 6 inches deep, with its surface 1 to 2 inches below ground level so that it won't be exposed. Since the footing won't be visible, you don't have to worry about making it attractive. Let the concrete cure overnight before laying the stone.

FIGURE 1: **Cross-Section View of Aboveground Fire Pit**

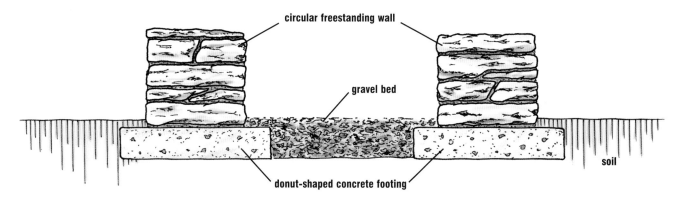

circular freestanding wall

gravel bed

soil

donut-shaped concrete footing

■ Building the Footing for a Belowground Fire Pit

The walls of a belowground fire pit are very similar to a small circular retaining wall (see figure 2). The bottom of a belowground fire pit wall should be about 12 to 18 inches below the earth's surface. Dig 4 to 6 inches deeper than the bottom of the wall for the footing. The footing should be 4 to 6 inches wider on each side than the fire pit wall. For example, if your fire pit is 18 inches below the ground and 14 inches wide, dig a circle 22 inches deep and 22- to 26-inches wide. Use marking spray to mark the diameter of your wall on the ground. This will give you enough room to play with different-size stones if needed. Refer to page 64 for directions on building footings. Pour the footing 4 to 6 inches deep. Add a couple of inches of gravel for fill in the center.

Laying the Stone

Once the footing has cured, spread a ½- to 1-inch layer of mortar on it and begin laying the stone as if you were building a freestanding or retaining wall, depending on whether your fire pit will be above or below ground. Begin with a row of stones and alternate courses from one side of the wall to the other. Push the stone into the mortar and pack it around the base of your first course. You can start with either the interior or exterior side at the base of your fire pit. Use one stone, when possible, to span the entire width of the wall. After the first course is set, pack mortar between the stones, both on the outside edge and in between. If you're building a jointed-style wall, follow the directions on page 90. For the dry-stack style, refer to page 87. Both styles will work on this project. A fire pit above ground, however, needs to be attractive on both sides, so manipulate each stone accordingly.

Laying the Capstones

As with any kind of wall you build, the cap is perhaps the most important part. Leave a level surface about 3 to 4 inches from the top of the wall for a cap, depending on the thickness of stone you're using. Pull a string to use as a gauge to create the straight top. Cut the edges of the capstones for nice, smooth curves on top. Leave a ½ - to 1-inch joint between the capstones for grouting. For a more detailed look at setting capstones, refer to page 88.

Allow the fire pit to dry for several days before building a fire. Then it's time to gather some sticks and open a bag of marshmallows.

FIGURE 2: **Cross-Section View of Belowground Fire Pit**

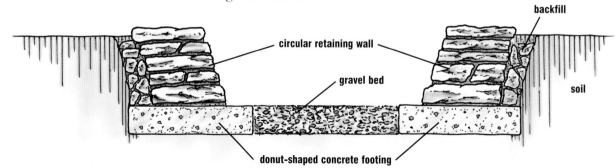

backfill

circular retaining wall

gravel bed

soil

donut-shaped concrete footing

Fire Pit on a Granite Slab

The homeowners hired me to build this fire pit on a large granite slab on the property. The original plan was for a belowground fire pit. Small holes were drilled into the piece of granite, and then the center was knocked out with a sledgehammer to create the opening for a pit.

I decided to raise the bottom of the pit and add a mortared rock wall to it. The wall made a good place to rest your feet when sitting in chairs around the fire, and it masked the hole in the center of the granite slab. I tied in the fire pit with the rest of the stonework on the house by using the same stones.

In a sense, this fire pit captures the best of both above- and belowground fire pits. The pit is a little deeper since it's both below ground and above ground, allowing the homeowners to build a larger fire. The stonework adds texture to the smooth, granite surface. Follow the instructions for building the walls of an aboveground fire pit if you want to add walls to an existing belowground fire pit. You may need to add extra gravel to raise the bottom of the pit a bit.

Fireplaces

What could be more satisfying than spending a cold winter's night cozied up to a warm, flickering fire in a stone fireplace? Answer: almost nothing—except doing the same in front of a fireplace that you've built yourself, stone by carefully placed stone. A stone fireplace adds presence and warmth to any room—from a living room or bedroom to a covered porch or patio. It has a magical appeal, and building one for yourself adds an entirely new dimension to that magic. What's more, modern techniques have made building a stone fireplace much easier today than in the past.

In the old days, fireplaces were made of nothing more than rock and mortar and were the only viable source of heat in a house. Although they were inefficient, if you had a large firebox and a heaping woodpile you could count on having at least one warm room in your home.

Modern fireplaces, unlike their predecessors, usually are not solid-stone and mortar structures and usually are not built entirely by a stonemason. Instead, the working portion of the fireplace has already been installed by a carpenter or block mason and usually consists of a cement-block or wood-sheathed chimney built around a metal or ceramic flue liner, and a firebox made of firebricks or a metal insert. Gone are the days when the stonemason has to worry about flue liners, throat diameters, dampers, and such. These days the stonemason's role in building a fireplace merely involves veneering over the cement block or wood of a newly constructed fireplace or the brick of an existing fireplace.

If you're just getting started in mortared stonework and have your heart set on a stone fireplace you've built by hand, chances are you'll be setting out to cover over an ordinary-looking brick fireplace or a drywall-sheathed wall that already exists in your home. That's what I show you how to do in detail on the next few pages. If you're having a new fireplace built from scratch and intend to veneer it with stone, you'll be working on top of the new structure's cement-block or wood surface as opposed to brick, but the process is the same.

Veneering an Existing Fireplace

Tools

In addition to the Basic Tool List on page 16, you'll need a framing square. Also, for wood sheathing or drywall, you'll need a moisture barrier such as 30-weight roofing felt, staple gun, staples, wall ties, and 8-penny nails. For veneering a masonry surface, you'll need wall ties and 1-inch concrete nails.

Mortar Recipe

Refer to the recipe for Mortar Mix for Dry-Stack Style on page 41 for dry-stack stonework or the Jointed-Style Mortar Mix recipe on that same page for jointed stonework.

Choosing Your Stone

A stone fireplace veneer can add tons of extra weight to the floor and wall, so you'll need to choose your stone carefully. If your fireplace is above the ground floor and there's not a strong chimney foundation, you'll need to use manufactured stone or a lightweight thin-veneer ("stick-on") stone. These stones are much lighter than the natural stone used for thick veneer, and the building technique used with them shifts much of the weight from the floor to the wall.

If the fireplace is on the ground level, or if you have a strong block or brick chimney foundation to support an upper-level fireplace, you can veneer with natural stone. If you're not sure about the structural makeup of your house and its ability to bear the finished fireplace's full weight, consult with a professional. Natural stone is heavier than manufactured stone, and it also requires more labor. On the other hand, shaping and placing your own rocks for a fireplace is remarkably satisfying. A perfect fireplace is a direct result of the time and patience you spend with each rock.

You can use almost any kind of stone—from cobblestone to ashlar—to build a fireplace. We covered our brick fireplace with a thick veneer of Virginia fieldstone (photo 1). Thick veneers need to be somewhere between 6 and 8 inches deep to provide adequate room for stones and mortar backfill. For thick veneer, medium to small stones work well as long as they're at least two inches thinner than the veneer space, leaving you enough room to pack mortar behind them. If you're sticking thin stones to the wall, the veneer will be much smaller. I don't recommend using stones thicker than two inches when applying a thin veneer.

The firebox was already small in this fireplace, so I had to be careful not to make it even smaller when I added a hearth to the floor. Flagstones 1 to 2 inches thick work perfectly for veneering hearths set directly on the floor or even on raised hearths. Don't use flagstones thinner than 1 inch; they're brittle and break easily when you set them. Also, you need something solid here in case you drop a log on the fireplace. If you have room to raise the hearth, any stone will work as long as it's fairly smooth on top, flat, and you have enough room to set the stone in mortar. Decide how much room you have to work with before you settle on the thickness of your stones. If you have enough room to raise the hearth 4 to 5 inches, thicker stones look better.

Getting Ready

First you need to decide whether you want to add a thin or a thick veneer to your fireplace, keeping in mind the strength of your floor and also that a thin veneer will make your new fireplace extend about 2 inches further out on each side, while a thick veneer will make it 6 to 8 inches larger. With the fireplace featured, I knew the chimney foundation could support a thick veneer, but I also had to determine if there was enough room between

the sides of the existing fireplace and the windows on either side. I figured on the new fireplace extending out 9 to 10 inches at the windows, since that's where my cantilevered mantel was located. It fit, and I thought the room could handle the effect of a thick veneer. You should carefully consider your own situation, though: An additional 6 to 8 inches added to a fireplace in a small living room might not seem like much, but trust me, you'll notice the difference.

Once you decide on thick or thin veneer, use tape to mark the outside dimensions of your new fireplace. This will serve as both an outline to help you lay stone and protection for the wall's surface.

Use a level to make sure the surface you're working on is plumb before you start. If it isn't, rather than using a tape measure to measure off the existing fireplace to the face of your stonework each time, you'll need to use your level to plumb the face of your stone veneer as you work your way up.

When looking directly at a fireplace, one of the first things people will notice is whether the corners form straight vertical lines. The best way to get straight corners is to pull strings to use as guides before you start (see Pulling Strings for Straight Corners, page 90). If you prefer the less formal, uneven corners of the dry-stack style I used with the fireplace here, don't bother with strings but do make sure each side of the fireplace is symmetrical and balanced as you lay your stone—stand back and let your eye be the judge every few feet. Instead of pulling strings, you can also use your level to plumb each cornerstone you set, but pulling strings makes the process go quicker.

Before you begin building, attach wall ties to the fireplace's brick surface (photo 2). The best place to nail them is between the joints. If you're veneering a drywall or wood-sheathed wall rather than a brick one, it's important to cover the wall with roofing felt or another type of moisture barrier to prevent the moisture in the mortar from weakening or rotting the sheathing. A moisture barrier can be attached to the wall horizontally with staples, overlapping each piece by about 4 inches (see page 75 for more detailed instructions).

Tape around the area you'll be veneering with any kind of masking or painter's tape. (Don't use duct tape, as it's sometimes difficult to remove.) After you've taped the edges, lay plastic, plywood, or another kind of protection to cover the floors. If you're planning to paint nearby walls or refinish the floor, it's always best to wait until after you've finished the stonework.

The house where this fireplace is located was in the process of being remodeled. Since I did the stonework before the hardwood floors were refinished, I just stacked my stones on plywood and worked directly on the floor. Small scratches were sanded down in the refinishing, but I was careful not to drop stones or hit them with a hammer on the floor.

Understanding the Parts of a Fireplace

Before you begin, refer to the illustration below (figure 1) to familiarize yourself with the names of the different parts of a fireplace. Select your cornerstones first—they're the most important stones you'll need when building a fireplace. (Remember, you'll need corners on the outside edges of the fireplace and also up the edges of the firebox.) Once I've selected my cornerstones, I set them aside so that I don't accidentally use them for something else.

FIGURE 1: **Parts of a Fireplace**

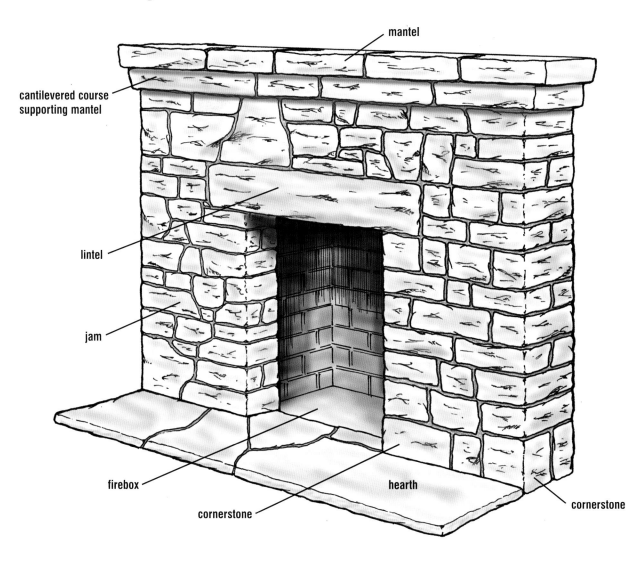

mantel

cantilevered course
supporting mantel

lintel

jam

firebox

cornerstone

hearth

cornerstone

FIGURE 2: **Veneering to the Wall**

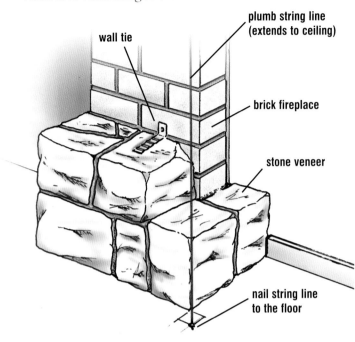

- plumb string line (extends to ceiling)
- wall tie
- brick fireplace
- stone veneer
- nail string line to the floor

■ Building the Jams and Setting the Lintel

To begin veneering the fireplace, start on one side of the firebox. These sections, called the jams, are the most difficult part of a fireplace to build because you don't have a lot of room to work with. Spread a thin layer of mortar on the floor, and set a cornerstone. After you get it plumb and set, set another corner on the other side of the same jam, and then lay your first course by filling in between with stones. Pack mortar behind each stone. You want to completely fill the outside edge of the fireplace with stone at each corner. You can do this either by using a thick stone to make the return on the outside corner or by simply putting another stone behind the cornerstone to fill the void (figure 2). This fireplace sits flat against the wall. In some cases, however, fireplaces extend out from the wall by as much as 3 feet. If your fireplace extends out from the wall, lay a course of stone on the side of the fireplace after you lay a course on the front. This will keep all the corners tied in. (For more information on building strong corners, refer to page 84.)

Continue this process up both sides of your firebox, remembering to fold wall ties over the stone and mortar. Unlike stone columns, where you need to build up all four sides one course at a time, it's acceptable to completely finish one side of a fireplace before you begin laying the other one. Overlap large corner faces over narrow corner faces after each course, so you always cross vertical joints.

Stop when you reach the top of the firebox. Use a level to make sure each jam is the same height (photo 3). If the jams aren't the same height, use a brick hammer to tap down the stones until the jams are level with each other (photo 4). You'll need to have the jams on both sides established and dried for at least one day before you set the lintel.

▌ Choosing the Lintel

Next, you'll cross the tops of the jams with a lintel. The role of a lintel is to provide a shelf on which to stack the stones that go above the firebox. I used a 6-inch-thick piece of stone as the lintel for the fireplace in the photos, but since stone lintels can be hard to find, you can use a piece of steel angle iron instead (photo 5). There's really no functional difference between the two types: it's largely a matter of preference and convenience. Using a steel lintel (available at most masonry supply stores and lumberyards) to bridge the stones across the firebox is probably easier than finding and shaping a lintel stone. Make sure the angle iron is at least 5 inches wide on the bottom and at least 3 inches wide on the back. Steel or stone lintels should extend over the jams at least 4 inches on each side. If you choose to use a stone lintel, it should be at least 4 inches thick. Check that the height of your lintel won't interfere with the location of your fireplace's mantel and mantel supports, if there are any.

If you're using a steel lintel, make sure the bottom shelf is slightly less than the distance between the face of your stones and the wall, so that the edge of the lintel won't stick out beyond the stonework. That's why I recommend a lintel with a bottom shelf that's 5 inches. This will allow for a 1-inch overhang if your veneer is 6 inches. If you're using a stone lintel, it can be 6 inches because you want the face of it to be flush with the stonework. I don't recommend altering the length of it unless you're really good at using a chisel. Since they're so long and thin, they can be brittle when hit with a hammer.

▌ Adding the Lintel

Dry set your lintel in place without mortar first to check its position and to see if it fits tightly. If you need to trim the lintel, do this before you set it in mortar. Once you're happy with the way it's set, take the lintel off the fireplace and spread a thin layer of mortar on the inside corner of each jam. Set the lintel back in place (photo 6). Ideally, you want your stone lintel to be as thick as the veneer so mortar doesn't fall through a gap between the back of the lintel and the brick of the fireplace. But perfect stone lintels are hard to come by. If there's a gap behind your lintel, wedge thin stones or metal flashing behind it to keep mortar from falling out before it hardens.

■ Adding the Rest of the Stone and the Mantel

Once your lintel has cured and you're satisfied that it's secure, continue setting stone, using the same pattern and technique you used when working on the jams, until you reach the spot for your mantel. To ensure you'll have enough room to set the mantel on top of the existing fireplace, you'll need to make the new veneer go a little higher. This will give you enough clearance to set the mantel on top. For safety reasons (and to follow code in most areas), the bottom of the mantel should be at least 12 inches away from the top of the firebox. As a good rule of thumb, the top of the mantel should be about eye level, or slightly above it.

This fireplace's mantel consists of two courses of stone (each cantilevered out 1 to 2 inches from the previous course) rather than a traditional wood mantel with mantel supports. (See the sidebar Mantel Supports & Wood Mantels on page 148 for a discussion of other types of mantels.) Building this mantel will be similar to laying two courses of capstones.

■ Laying the First Course of Mantel Stone

Once the last course of stone before the mantel has been set and leveled off, you can begin laying your first cantilevered course of stones. Start with a cornerstone, which should have two sides that form a 90° angle and shouldn't be more than 3 or 4 inches thick, to keep it proportional with the rest of the fireplace. Set the first corner, making sure it cantilevers out 1 to 2 inches from the course below (photos 7 and 8). Lay a couple more

stones adjacent to it, making them level with the cornerstone. When you have laid enough stones to span the distance to the other corner with a level, move to the other corner and set another cornerstone with a 90° angle, making sure this stone extends out the same distance as the first cornerstone. Check that the corners are level with each other (photo 9).

9

11

Use this same method to fill in between the two corners with horizontal flat stones that are the same thickness as the cornerstones. Tap each stone into a 1-inch mortar bed with a rubber mallet (photo 10). Pack around each stone with mortar to make it secure. Pack mortar behind the stones all the way to the wall. After all the voids and cracks are full, use your trowel to spread a layer of mortar on top of this course so that you can set the final course on top.

10

▌Laying the Top Course of Mantel Stone

All the stones for the top course need to be of equal thickness, but they don't need to be the same thickness as the stones in the course below. (As you can see in photo 11 and the project photos, I used slightly thicker stones for the top course.) Just as you did with the prior course, start by setting the two cornerstones that cantilever out 1 to 2 inches from the course below, and then fill in between with horizontal stones. Pay closer attention to the appearance of the top of this course, since it will be visible. Use flat, smooth stones and keep the mortar joints on top ½ to 1 inch wide. Set each stone with a rubber mallet, and use a four-foot level to make sure the top is even. Use some of your leftover mortar to grout between the joints with a tuck pointer. Let the mortar dry and scratch out with the blade of the tuck pointer (see page 159 for more on grouting). Use a whiskbroom to sweep away the excess.

If you're not going to build a hearth or you're going to use the fireplace's original hearth, then you're all done. Be sure to let the mortar cure for at least five days before building a fire in your new fireplace.

If the bottom of your firebox is level with the finished floor, as was the case with the brick fireplace in the photos, you might want to add an attractive hearth by simply laying flat hearthstones on the floor. This is the easiest type of do-it-yourself hearth for someone just starting out in mortared stonework.

Building the Hearth

■ Preparing the Surface for the Hearth

Since cement won't bond to wood, you'll need to nail metal lath to a wood floor before you begin building your hearth (photos 12 and 13). Lath will help keep the hearth in place. To prevent moisture from damaging the wood, attach a moisture barrier to the floor with staples before adding the lath. You don't need metal lath if you're laying stone on a concrete floor or a floor-level concrete hearth like the one in this project. Because I increased the size of the hearth a little on the sides and the front, I did attach lath to those places on the hardwood floor.

Before applying mortar, outline the shape of the hearth with a pencil, and tape the outside edge so you don't stain the floor with concrete. This will protect the surface of a finished floor and also define your workspace.

You can vary the dimensions of the hearth to achieve the look that works best for your particular fireplace and room. Hearths typically extend to the outside edges of the jams, but make yours whatever length you like. You can cut the hearth's corners at 45° angles, round them off, or make the edges jagged and irregular. To stick with the overall shape of the original fireplace I was veneering, I planned a rectangular, straight-edged hearth that was the same width as the fireplace.

■ Choosing and Shaping Hearthstones

Once you choose flat stones for the hearth, set aside the ones with straight edges for the front and sides. If you don't have any with perfectly straight edges, use a pencil and a straightedge to mark a straight line (photo 14), and make an edge with your brick hammer.

Since the fireplace in the photos wasn't originally designed to have a hearth, I didn't have much room to build one, so I decided to use thin stones, about 2 inches thick. Your hearthstones should be flat and somewhat smooth on top; although, if your hearth, like the one I built, is only slightly raised and won't function as a seat, you can use stones with more texture.

You should also think about the stones you'll be adding to the bottom of the firebox—you don't want to reduce the size of the firebox too much. I laid thin stones all the way to the back of the firebox, but you can instead end your hearthstones at the front edge.

■ Laying the Hearthstones

Begin laying the stones by first spreading a thin layer of mortar over a small section on one corner (photo 15). You don't want to spread it over the entire area, as it might dry before you set all the stones. Use your rubber mallet to set your first stone in this mortar bed. As you can see, I used a large stone for the first corner (photo 16). Smaller stones on horizontal surfaces such as this tend to look pieced together. Use the same method to set the other cornerstone, and check to make sure the two cornerstones are level (photo 17). If they're not, remove the stone and adjust the thickness of your mortar bed. Lay the rest of the hearth's border with your straight-edged stones, and then fill in the center with smaller stones. Let the hearthstones dry before you grout them.

After the hearth cures, grout the joints (see page 159), and sweep away the excess mortar. Remove any tape around the hearth and fireplace. Use a vacuum to clean the mortar dust and a damp rag to clean any mortar residue left on the floor. It will take at least 24 hours for the mortar to harden, but wait at least five days before building a fire in the fireplace.

Mantel Supports & Wood Mantels

Stone mantel supports, which project out from the fireplace wall to provide support for the mantel, are generally used in fireplaces that extend to the ceiling so that the weight of the fireplace holds them down. You can install mantel supports on a short fireplace, but I recommend attaching the supports and mantel to the wall before you lay the stone. The same goes for a thin veneer fireplace: Since the stonework won't support mantel supports or mantels, you must attach them before the fireplace is built. Here's some basic information to use if this type of mantel fits your situation better than the course of stone we used.

Positioning the Mantel Supports

The top of your mantel supports should be no less than 12 inches above the bottom of the lintel. The top of the mantel should be at about eye level, so you may need to adjust the height of your mantel supports to take into account the thickness of your mantel. Position the mantel supports so they're centered above the jams, or between the center of the jams and the edge of the firebox, on both sides. I find it easiest to draw a picture of where the mantel supports need to go on the wall. Measure the dimensions of your mantel supports so you can make an accurate mark. Use a level to make sure the marks are level with each other.

I recommend projecting the mantel supports out from the stonework about 8 inches. This will allow you to overhang a 10-inch mantel by 2 inches. These supports should extend in the back all the way to the wall to which you are veneering, so that they can be tied in strongly with the other stones (figure 3).

Choosing Mantel Support Stones

Mantel support stones should have a flat top. If yours don't, use a chop saw to make the tops flat. The easiest way to size the stones is to use a chop saw to cut off the backs of the stones. You can also use wood mantel supports or pieces of antique timbers in place of stone.

Adding the Mantel Supports

Continue building the fireplace above the lintel and stop when you get to your mantel support line on the wall. Before you position the supports on the wall, you'll need something to temporarily hold them in place while you build the remainder of the fireplace. Measure the distance between the bottom of the support and the floor, and cut a piece of wood (such as a 2x4) to that length. Use this as a support until you get some stones stacked on top. (I often leave the 2x4s in place until I'm finished with the base of the fireplace and ready to build the hearth.) When you get your mantel supports level and have your 2x4s in place, you can continue building the rest of the fireplace to the ceiling.

Placing the Mantel

If you're using a wood mantel with your fireplace, finish the mantel as desired before you place it on the mantel supports so that you don't stain the stones. If you've set the mantel supports correctly, the mantel should sit level and secure on the supports. You don't need to attach it to the supports. If the supports are not level, or if one side of the mantel is thicker, you can adjust by putting a thin layer of mortar on top of one mantel support. If you're using a stone mantel, have it cut to size by a professional, or use a chop saw. Check with your local stone supplier to find a stonecutter.

FIGURE 3: **Mantel Support**

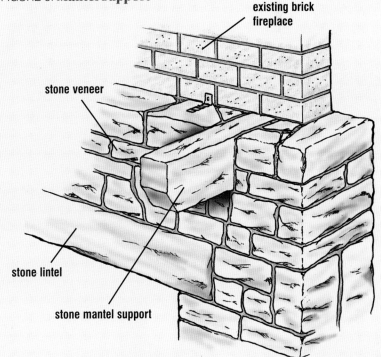

existing brick fireplace

stone veneer

stone lintel

stone mantel support

Keystones & Soldiers

If your fireplace has an arched lintel, it makes sense, geometrically speaking, to use stones known as a keystone and soldiers to create the shape of an arch. A keystone is the wedge-shaped stone at the highest point of an arch. Soldiers are usually slightly smaller vertical stones, on either side of the keystone, which connect to the other stonework on the jams. Today, keystones and soldiers are primarily used for aesthetic reasons; they don't serve a structural function in stonework but accentuate the fireplace's subtle arch and draw your eyes to the opening.

The keystone is usually a larger, trapezoid-shaped shiner placed with the narrow side down. When you're cutting this stone, be sure to make a good seat so the keystone won't shift or fall off the steel lintel. The easiest way to make a keystone is to find a large fieldstone—close to keystone size so you won't have to chisel much—with a smooth, flat bottom, or seat. Use a straightedge and pencil to mark the exact shape of the keystone you want. Use your hand-set chisel to chip away the edges until you hit your pencil mark. You typically want to place a keystone vertically rather than horizontally. I have cut a keystone as tall as 20 inches and made one as small as 8 inches. The idea is to make the size proportional to the overall size of your fireplace.

The stones standing vertically beside the keystone are known as soldiers. To determine how many to make, measure the width of your firebox opening. Your soldiers should be about 4 to 8 inches wide and around 6 to 10 inches tall. A good rule of thumb is that they should be no taller than the center keystone, and preferably a couple of inches shorter. Again, mark your stones with a pencil and use a hand-set chisel to shape them. If you're working with manufactured stone, order the keystone and soldiers with the rest of the stone. Your supplier should have various size and design options.

To set your keystone and soldiers, spread a thin layer of mortar across the lintel and set your keystone first. Use a shim or wedge if the stone doesn't have a balanced and stable seat. Line your soldiers across each side of the lintel and pack mortar behind each of them, including the lintel. Make sure they don't fall off the lintel. If they move, hold them with one hand while you pack mortar with the other until you're sure they're in place. Your soldiers should extend to the end of the lintel on each side; then you can continue with your regular pattern of stonework to the edge of the fireplace corner.

Patios & Walkways

With about a weekend of work, you can transform a ho-hum surface into an inviting flagstone-paved patio or walkway. Perhaps your backyard has one of those generic slabs that were so popular a few decades ago. Or maybe the walkway to your front door is an uninspiring stretch of gray concrete. Mortared flagstone can turn drab patios or utilitarian walkways into features that are both useful and attractive.

While many types of paving material are available these days, it's hard to beat stone for looks and durability. The natural beauty of stone constuction can provide an pleasing link between your home and the outdoors.

In this chapter I teach you how to use flagstone as a horizontal veneer to cover a concrete patio or walkway using a scramble pattern that gives you the freedom to design the stonework as you go. If you love the thought of a stone patio or path, but you don't have a preexisting one to veneer, you can hire someone to pour a concrete pad for you or follow my instructions for building bases starting on page 68. Sound like too much work or money? I've still got you covered. I'll show you a technique that allows you to lay a flagstone walkway or patio without a concrete slab.

Veneering a Concrete Patio or Walkway

The instructions that follow describe the method I used to veneer the patio in the photos. The only difference in veneering a concrete walkway is that walkways are generally more curved and longer than a patio, so you might have to spend a little more time cutting the edges. The most important steps to consider before you begin the walkway are to make sure the existing walkway has the correct pitch to shed water and to use string lines to keep the flagstone surface smooth. (See Establishing a Base's Pitch on page 69 for more information.)

Tools and Materials

In addition to the Basic Tool List (page 16), you'll need a broom or a gas-powered blower. If you're going to use wet grout instead of dry (see the sidebar Wet Grout Method, page 160), you'll also need a grout bag.

Mortar Recipe

Refer to the recipe for Mortar Mix for Horizontal Flagstone and Grout on page 41.

Choosing Your Stone

Flagstone is a flat stone used mostly on horizontal surfaces, such as floors, patios, walkways, and driveways. The gray flagstone used in the walkway project (page 161) and the colored flagstone used in the patio project were both 1½- to 2½-inch-thick sandstone, which came from Tennessee. This colored flagstone is generally sold in ½- to 3-inch-thick pieces. I don't recommend using flagstone less than 1 inch thick; it's brittle and breaks when set with a mallet, and it makes a less-durable surface. Generally, the thicker the flagstone, the stronger the stonework, but honestly, 3-inch-thick stones are heavy and might be awkward for you to set. I recommend using stones that are between 1 and 2 inches thick. Stick with flagstone that has a little texture so you won't slip when it gets wet.

Flagstone is easiest and most cost-effective to lay when you use a scramble pattern with small, medium, and large stones, along with various colors chosen for an even and balanced pattern. To keep your mortar joints consistent, be prepared to cut each piece of flagstone, fitting the pieces together like a puzzle. Random pieces of flagstone are sold on a pallet by weight.

If you want to curve the patio or give it some shape, stick with a medium-density flagstone such as sandstone, so it will be easier to lay curved edges. Dense flagstone is harder to cut and typically doesn't break just where you want it to.

Determining the Amount of Stone Needed

If you're using 1- to 1½-inch-thick flagstone, you'll get an average of 120 to 150 square feet per ton if you use almost every piece. If you pick through the pallet and use only the perfectly flat stones that aren't split in the middle (which is what I recommend), you'll get about 100 to 120 square feet per ton. With a 2- to 3-inch-thick stone, you'll get only about 50 to 75 square feet per ton. Most stone suppliers will deliver your flagstone, and most trucks bring a forklift or boom to unload the pallets. If the flagstone is soft, such as sandstone or limestone, it shouldn't be dumped on a hard surface. If you don't have someone to mechanically unload it for you, do it yourself manually. In the event you have to dump the flagstone, dump it on a few empty pallets so that the stones don't break.

The colored flagstone used for our patio came from Tennessee.

Getting Ready

The old concrete base you'll be covering doesn't have to be aesthetically pleasing, but it does need to be fairly solid. Smaller cracks and chips in the pad are acceptable, but make sure there aren't large cracks or sections that are broken or have severely deteriorated. The pad also needs to be clean and free of oil, dust, or efflorescence for the mortar to adhere properly. Use a pressure washer or muriatic acid or another heavy-duty concrete cleaner if needed. Check with your local masonry supply company for product availability, and follow the manufacturer's instructions and safety precautions.

■ Checking the Pad's Pitch

A patio or walkway must be pitched so that water doesn't stand between the edges or pour into an adjacent building's foundation. Existing concrete patios should already have the correct pitch (¼-inch pitch per linear foot), but you need to check to be certain. (See Establishing a Base's Pitch, on page 69.) If your slab doesn't have ¼-inch pitch per linear foot, ⅛ inch will work. If it has no pitch, you'll need to establish the correct pitch with a string line and a line level following the instructions in the sidebar, and then correct the pitch of the finished stone surface by adjusting the mortar bed as you lay the stone.

Remember that once you pave the concrete slab, its finished height will be higher, so plan accordingly. If your patio slab butts up against a door to the house, for instance, you'll need to make sure that the paved slab pitches away from the house.

Pulling Strings

To begin veneering a slab patio, first determine the height of your finished surface and pull a small grid of strings to make laying the stone easier. This will give you a frame of reference when trying to keep the flagstone surface smooth and correctly pitched (photos 1 and 2). To pull strings, drive stakes into the ground on each side of the patio, leaving them a few inches above the finished level of the patio on each side. Tie nylon string taut between the two stakes.

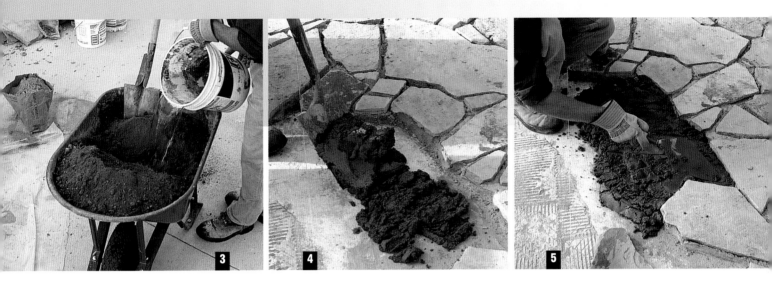

Mixing and Spreading the Mortar

If you're new to laying flagstone, mix only one batch of mortar at a time to prevent it from drying out as you set the stone (photo 3). (See page 42 for instructions on mixing flagstone mortar.) Once you gain experience and begin laying the flagstone at a faster pace, you might consider mixing more than one batch at a time, since you'll use it quickly.

Using a shovel, spread mortar onto the concrete pad in about a 4-foot-square area (photo 4). Start at the back of the patio so you don't step on the stones after they're set. Make this mortar bed about ½ to 1 inch thicker than you actually need, so you can tap the flagstone into place. Use a trowel to spread the mortar and to smooth the bed before setting the stone (photo 5). Depending on the thickness of the stone, you might have to adjust the depth of the mortar bed for thicker or thinner stones. If you've made the right mortar, you should be able to work the stones into place by tapping them with a rubber mallet (photo 6). If the mortar is too wet, you'll need to check the stones frequently to make sure they haven't shifted after they're in place. If it's too dry and the rubber mallet doesn't seem to set the stones, pour a little water on the mortar bed and chop it with your trowel until it's wet enough.

Laying the Stones

If you're creating a square or rectangular patio, use your stones with straight edges on the borders of the patio. If you're laying a curved patio or walkway, look for naturally curved stones or shape stones with a hammer. When you're laying a walkway, start with the edges and then lean over the edge stones to fill in the middle. For a patio, start with one side and lay the edges before filling in the middle about three quarters of the way to the other side, leaving a path in the middle to walk through. Then lay the other edge and lean over and fill in the gap.

Use large stones with straight edges on the sides, and then fill in the middle with smaller stones, but save some large stones without straight edges to work into the middle of the patio, as they break up the monotony of the smaller stones. Use a sharp brick hammer to alter the shapes of the stones as needed. Laying flagstone is like putting together the pieces of a puzzle. The more time you spend making the stones fit together, the better it will look.

Tightly fitting the stones together with mortar joints is the most difficult part of laying flagstone, although it can easily be the most rewarding aspect if done right. Like so much of stonework, it gets easier and easier with practice. As you start with larger stones on the edges and work your way toward the center, filling in with stones, look for pieces that have an edge similar to the stone you're fitting against. If you're filling a hole, make a mental note of the space you're trying to fill, and find a close match in the pile. If you need to cut to make a stone fit, overlap the stone you're going to fill in with over the

stone that's already set, and mark where you need to cut the new stone. Often, it comes down to trial and error: Cut the stone into the shape you think will fit and try it. You will almost always have to take it out and try again. It's not unusual to have to do this three or four times before you get it right. Don't set the stone in mortar until it's right.

As you're setting the stones, remember to keep the mortar joints between them ½ to 1 inch thick. Before you get too far along, use a 4- or 6-foot level to make sure the flagstone surface has the right pitch and each stone is flush (photo 7). Keep an eye on the strings, and make sure they don't sag—they should be taut throughout the entire process. Keep a level handy and use it frequently. If it's a really hot day, use the mortar within one hour of making it; otherwise, you'll need to throw a couple of wet empty mortar bags or a piece of plywood over the wheelbarrow to shade the mortar.

At the end of the day, use your trowel to cut the mortar that bulges out from under the stones' outside edges flush with the sides. Then use your pointing trowel to rake out all the mortar joints around each stone. The mortar from the mortar bed will rise between the stones when you tap them with a mallet. Rake them out at least 1 inch below the surface of the stones so the grout will be able to adhere better. Don't walk on the flagstone for 24 hours before and after grouting. If the project is large, rake the joints after you set each stone so you don't have to walk on them before the mortar cures.

Grouting the Joints

There are two ways to grout the joints: wet grouting and dry grouting. Wet grouting, which requires making extremely wet mortar and squirting it into the joints with a grout bag, takes much longer to dry and requires more steps than the dry-grout method, which consists of manually packing a dry mortar mixture into the joints with a pointing trowel. Both require placing mortar in the joints, allowing the mortar to dry, and then scratching the joints with a pointing trowel and brushing the flagstone off. Which method you should choose depends on how much time you have and the immediate weather forecast. Wet grouting (which is a lot like applying icing to a cake) is just plain tricky to get the hang of. I recommend dry grouting for beginners. It does take more work, but it's easier to do, and you don't have to wait as long for the mortar to dry before you begin scratching out. If you're up for a challenge, see the sidebar Wet-Grout Method (on page 160) for instructions. Whichever method you choose, allow the flagstones' mortar to dry overnight before you begin grouting, remember to keep a pair of knee pads handy, and don't step on the joints until the grout completely dries.

▪ Dry-Grout Method

This technique doesn't require as much time waiting for the mortar to dry, but the process of packing each joint by hand is a bit more tedious. Refer to page 41 for the dry-grout mortar recipe. Using one hand or a trowel to scoop the mortar, spread a layer across the joint and work the mortar into the joint with a pointing trowel (photo 8). Push it down as hard as you can. Add more until the mortar is mounded slightly above the surface of the stones. Take your time and keep the amount of mortar smeared on the edges of the stones to a minimum. Continue grouting in this manner until all the joints are full. Press your finger into the joints to make sure the mortar is packed very firmly. If some of the mortar pops out, repack the joints with leftover mortar.

Periodically check to make sure the joints you've grouted aren't too dry. If they are, it will be much more difficult to scratch them back. After the mortar is dry to the touch, scratch the joints flush with the surface of the stones, using the horizontal edge of a pointing trowel or tuck pointer. The mortar should be powdery after you scratch it back. If it leaves a wet residue on the edges of the stones, it's not ready to be scratched.

If the mortar isn't used up within one hour, check it to make sure it's still wet enough to use. To test, grab a handful with one hand and throw it into the air. If it holds its shape, it's wet enough. If it breaks apart, add a small amount of water. When you finish scratching, sweep away the excess mortar (photo 9).

Wet-Grout Method

Use this technique only if you begin early on a day with no rain in the forecast for at least eight hours. It sometimes takes all day for wet grout to dry. Also, I don't recommend using this method on soft stone, such as sandstone or limestone, because it could permanently stain the edges of the stones. Refer to page 41 for the wet grout mortar recipe. Mix the mortar and then use a trowel to scoop some into a grout bag. Squeeze the bag to spread the mortar into the joints (the technique is similar to using a pastry bag to add icing to a cake). Apply enough mortar into the cracks so that it sits slightly above the surface of the stones. Periodically, go back to where you started and use the pointed end of your brick mason's trowel to press the mortar into the joints, but make sure no part of the grout in the joints is below the surface of the stones, as this will give water a place to sit. Continue grouting and troweling the joints until you fill all the cracks.

When finished, be prepared to wait at least several hours for the grout mortar to dry, depending on the temperature and the amount of direct sunlight on the patio. Once the mortar is dry to the touch, use a pointing trowel to scratch the joints flush with the surface of the stones. It should break and crumble away fairly easily. If it's too wet, wait a little longer. If it's too dry, you might find that using a flat hoe scratches it back more easily. After this initial scratch, the mortar joints should still be a little moist. You can tell by looking at the edges of the stones. You have basically removed the dry mortar from the top of the surface of the stones, leaving the mortar below the surface moist.

After you scratch the joints flush, wait at least one hour, and then use a steel brush to scratch away the mortar residue on the edges of the stones. The mortar should be dry enough that it turns into a fine powder. If it's still smearing on the edges of the stones, wait longer. After you finish scratching, use a broom or a gas or electric blower to remove the excess mortar.

Use a pointing trowel to scratch the joints flush with the surface of the stones.

Laying a Flagstone Walkway or Patio without a Slab

If you don't have a pre-existing concrete walkway or patio to veneer and you don't want to go to the trouble of pouring a slab, you can still lay a mortared-stone walkway or patio. With this technique you simply use an extra-thick mortar bed instead of a pad. It doesn't require more skill, just a little extra labor excavating the soil and making mortar. Other than that, you'll follow the directions in the previous sections to lay the stones and grout them.

The instructions that follow describe how I made the walkway in the photo above, but the process is essentially the same for a patio.

Laying the Stones

To make a walkway or patio with this method, you'll follow the same directions given for laying stones on a slab, except that you'll be making your pad as you go. Instead of spreading a thin layer of mortar as you would with a preexisting pad, spread a 4- or 5-inch-thick mortar bed and set your first course of stones, keeping the front edge straight (photo 2). Lay edges first, and then work your way into the middle, leaving a path to walk through.

Building a Walkway on Sloped Ground

While some pitch is needed for your structure to shed water, too much slope will be slippery when it gets wet. If you're laying a walkway on a slope, I recommend building it in tiers.

As you can see in photo 1, this was the case with the walkway I built for this project. The difference in height between the start of the path at the porch and the other end at the driveway was 18 inches. Since this project was only about 25 feet long, I felt like this was too much of a slope. A reasonable step is anywhere from 5 to 7 inches, so I decided to add two 6-inch steps to the path, ultimately making 3 tiers of walkway. I cut the risers in as I excavated (photo 3), spreading them out over the entire length of the path so the walkway wasn't ever much higher than the finished grade.

Excavating for a No-Slab Walkway or Patio

Begin by outlining the perimeter of the walkway or patio with marking spray, string, or a hose. Pull strings on each end of the walkway to use as a gauge to excavate the soil (you'll use the strings as a guide when laying the stones as well). Drive two stakes into the ground and pull the string taut between them. The string should be set just above the finished grade line. You want the surface of your finished walkway or patio to be slightly higher than ground level—if it's lower, it will hold water.

This no-slab technique requires a 4- to 5-inch mud bed (and gravel if the soil is soft). So dig out the soil about 5 to 6 inches below the string line, or 5 inches below the thickness of your stones (photo 1). Make sure you follow the outline while digging so the sides of the soil bank will contain the mortar bed. The soil on which you will lay the mortar bed and stones should be hard and compacted. If it is, you're ready to lay the stones. If the soil is soft or is fill dirt, you need to compact it or add gravel. If you have to dig a few inches to get below the fill dirt, make up the difference with gravel.

■ Laying Stones for Steps

If you're building a walkway with steps, when you reach the end of your first tier, use your level or a straightedge to mark a line across the stone, about 10 inches in front of the dirt step you dug (photo 4). This line will indicate where the first riser will go. Since my risers in this project were 6 inches tall, I stacked two 3-inch stones on top of each other for this course (photos 5–8). The top stones need to be large and flat since this is visible stone. You also want these first stones on the lip of the steps to be large, solid stones since they'll be subjected to the pressure of people stepping up onto them.

Finishing

Continue setting the stones and following the outline you dug, adding steps if necessary, until you get to the end of your path. Remember to use your level to make sure the walkway has the correct pitch. If you dig out a little too much soil, use flagstone chips to fill in the low spot so you don't have to make as much mortar (photo 9). If you need to make the top of your walkway higher than the thickness of one course of stones above ground level, stack two courses on the edges, so you don't see the side of the mortar bed (photo 10). Follow the directions on page 159 to grout the joints (photo 11).

Steps

By now you've seen how stone can be used to beautify the entrance to your property, add character to your living room, and spice up a drab surface such as a patio or walkway. Any realtor will tell you that one of the most important exterior features of your home is the entryway. This is the place that makes a first impression on guests and welcomes you and your family home. If you need steps to get from the outdoors to inside, you've got the perfect opportunity to let mortared stone work its magic.

The easiest way to make mortared stone steps is to veneer an existing set of poured concrete steps or to veneer a core of concrete blocks that have been laid for steps. The actual veneering for steps isn't any harder than for any of the other projects, but understanding how to get steps to start and end just where you want them to can be a little tricky. What can be hard to get the hang of at first is that veneering steps involves both horizontal and vertical stonework. The top portion of a step is called the tread. Veneering the treads is essentially the same as laying and grouting flagstones for a patio or a wall cap. The vertical portion of a step that's visible is called the riser. Veneering risers will be similar to veneering a concrete block wall. If you've tried your hand at some of the simpler projects in this book, veneering steps shouldn't be too big of a challenge, but, trust me, laying the block core for the steps is not a job for an amateur. If you don't already have a set of concrete steps to veneer, hire a building contractor or block mason to build the core for you.

In this chapter, I teach you to thick-veneer concrete block steps. I used the dry-stack style for the risers, but you can use the jointed style instead (refer to the instructions for jointed-style stonework on page 89). Whichever joint style you use for the risers, the treads will be flagstones laid with mortared joints.

Tools and Materials

See Basic Tool List on page 16.

Mortar Recipe

Refer to the recipe for Mortar Mix for Dry-Stack Style on page 41 for dry-stack stonework or the Mortar Mix for Jointed-Style recipe on that same page for jointed stonework.

Choosing Your Stone

Choose tread stones that are at least 8 inches deep, with straight edges for the front. Jagged and rough edges will create a trip hazard. The best type of stone to use for the treads is flagstone. Use a medium to dense stone for the treads since the steps will be getting a lot of wear and tear. Soft stones, such as limestone and soft sandstone, might deteriorate.

The treads should be relatively smooth, without large knots, cracks, or other irregularities that might create trip hazards. However, a tread that's too smooth might be slick when wet. Use your best judgment and find a happy medium. If you use a different type of stone for the tread than for the riser, have your stone yard help you find a close color match.

I used 2- to 4-inch-thick fieldstones for the risers in this project. Depending on the height of your riser, you can use one stone or several stacked stones to get the riser height you need. For instance, if your riser height is 7 inches and you're using 2-inch-thick flagstone for the treads, then the stones beneath the tread will need to be 5 inches high. You could use one 5-inch-high stone or stack two stones, one 2 inches and one 3 inches, on top of each other.

Treads will be subject to constant stress, so use a medium to dense stone.

Getting Ready

If you're veneering a set of existing concrete steps, you just need to make sure they're clean and sturdy. If you're starting from scratch, you'll need to hire a block mason to build the core (photo 1). Before your mason arrives to construct the core, clear the worksite and provide a clean place to work. This will make the process go much smoother. Also, be sure to tell him or her approximately how high you want the risers and how deep (the distance from the front to the back of the tread) you want the treads to be. You should also decide beforehand how wide you want the finished steps to be.

A 6 to 8 inch riser is comfortable for most people, though I prefer to keep them around 6 to 7 inches. The standard building code is generally around 7 inches; be sure to check this before you decide. Tread depth is up to you. I build treads anywhere from 12 to 18 inches deep. Eighteen inches is a bit much for short people, but 12 inches is a little short for people with large feet. Use another set of steps as a gauge for making your own.

You'll need to let the block mason know whether you want the top step to be level with the floor of the building or if you want to step up into the building—the decision is up to you. In the featured project, it might appear from looking at the concrete blocks (photo 1) that the homeowner would be stepping up into the house, but, as you can see in the project photo on the next page, I created a riser on top of the last step so the final tread would be level with the floor of the house.

The white material between the door and top block in the photo is a product used on vertical surfaces in new construction to provide protection from water and moisture. A strip of metal, aluminum or copper flashing is used to further increase water and moisture resistance on wood surfaces, especially under a door threshold. The flashing should start under the door threshold and fold down the wood sheathing about 4 or 5 inches. This will prevent water from entering the house under the doorframe, or threshold. Don't forget to add wall ties to the vertical sides of the block before you start veneering if your block mason hasn't done so.

Thick-Veneered Steps

Start at the Top

I prefer to start with the top step instead of the bottom, so I don't work on top of steps I just set. This also allows me err at the bottom, which is better than erring at the top. If you end up with a 3-inch step at the top and all of your other steps are 7 inches, you won't be able to correct your mistake. If you accidentally leave yourself with 3 inches for the bottom step, you can make up for the miscalculation by adding another step or adding fill to raise the soil.

All block masons are different, so sometimes you have to make do with whatever scenario you're left with. It helps to mark with a pencil where the top of each tread will be located (see figure 1). I had about a foot from the floor of the house to the top of the block work (photo 1). Since I knew I'd be using 2-inch-thick flagstone for the tread, that left me with about 10 inches for the first riser. Don't assume you'll be building this same amount for the next riser; it may vary depending on your situation. The instructions that follow assume you'll also be using 2-inch-thick flagstones for the treads. If you aren't, just remember to account for the thickness of your treads when you're building the risers.

Veneering the Sides

Now that you know where the top of your top riser will go, begin veneering the sides of the steps. Your front risers and treads will cross over these veneered sides. Use a trowel, shovel, and broom to make sure all debris is removed from the footing before spreading any mortar. Lay the stones 6 inches out from the concrete riser (photos 2 and 3). (I laid them dry-stack style, but you can use jointed style if you prefer.) Fill in with backfill or stone chips and mortar (photo 4).

FIGURE 1: **Cross-Section of Veneered Steps**

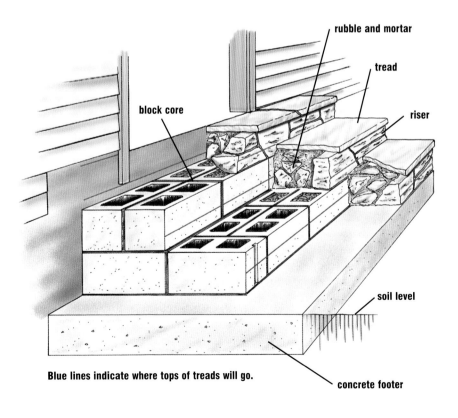

rubble and mortar

tread

block core

riser

soil level

concrete footer

Blue lines indicate where tops of treads will go.

Tying the Sides and Front Together

When you've veneered one side to the top of the block core, add mortar to the top block step, and then cross the vertical joint between the block and the side veneer with a cornerstone, tying it all together (photo 5). Veneer the other side of the concrete blocks, and then set another cornerstone that crosses the vertical joint between the block core and the side veneer on that other side.

Veneering the Top Riser

The top riser is a very thick veneer (which, as you can see in the photos, actually veneers the outside wall of the house) laid on the top concrete block step. To build this top riser, lay stones between the cornerstones, and then fill behind them with mortar and rubble (photo 6). Continue laying courses of stone by setting cornerstones—check to make sure you'll have enough room for the tread (photo 7). Fill in between with stones backed by mortar and rubble (photo 8). Continue adding cornerstones and courses until you reach the level where the tread goes (photo 9).

Laying the Top Tread

After you finish the riser, spread a mortar bed, and use a rubber mallet to set the two corner treads stones, using a stone with a 90° angle for each corner. The stones should have a ⅛- to ¼-inch pitch from the back to the front to shed water (photo 10), and both corner treads should be level with each other (photo 11). Finish the top tread by filling in between with stones with straight front edges. Dry-fit these stones to see if you need to chip away the back of any (photo 12). If you do, use a brick hammer (photos 13) to shape the stone before setting it (photo 14). Check each stone for proper pitch and to make sure they are level with each other, and leave a ½-inch mortar joint between each stone on the tread.

Scratching out the Joints

Scratch out the riser joints when they're ready, and sweep away the excess (see page 90 for more on scratching out joints). Leave the mortar joints on the treads alone for now.

Thin Veneer (or Stick-On) Steps

You might instead want to add thin-veneer (stick-on) stonework to your concrete steps. The advantage of thin veneer is that you'll greatly reduce the amount of stone needed. If you want to go this route, make sure you tell the block mason how much room to leave you. The treads will need 2 to 4 inches for stone and mortar. The risers and the sides of the steps will need 1 to 2 inches for mortar and stone, depending on the thickness of your stones. Leftover, thin pieces of flagstone work well for thin veneer on the risers, and they'll match the treads in color. The stick-on technique is explained on page 92.

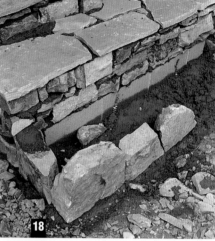

Veneering the Second and Third Steps

When you finish the top step, use your level and measure down 10 inches (or whatever amount works for your situation). This is where the top of your next tread will go. Build the sides up far enough for your treads and risers to cross the sides of the steps (photo 15). Follow the same method to build your second riser. Leave enough room to accommodate the 2-inch-thick tread, and make sure your riser is level (photo 16). When you get your riser leveled off, fill in with rubble and mortar and set a corner tread (photo 17). Set another corner tread and fill in between just like you did with the first step.

Follow the same instructions for the third step. Measure down 10 inches, and finish building the sides and the front of the riser; this level will be set on the footing (photo 18). Veneer this last riser, making sure your top course of stone and rubble is level. Then set your treads, starting with the corners and filling in between (photo 19).

Grouting the Tread Stones

If you can grout the treads without stepping on them, go ahead and do it now if they are somewhat dry. If they are still floating in wet mortar, wait until the next day. Follow the instructions on page 159 to grout the treads just as you would a flagstone patio (photos 20–22).

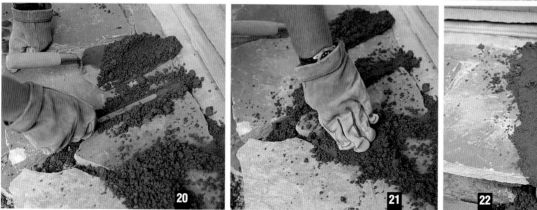

Steps in a Landscape without a Concrete Base

Unattractive, hard-to-traverse slopes are the bane of landscapers everywhere. Often the solution is a set of steps; mortared stone steps can open up an unused portion of your yard while adding a refining touch.

Mortared stone steps are permanent: they shed water and they won't settle and shift over time like dry-laid stone steps. Steps can be built into virtually any type of slope—they can be designed with flowing curves, zigzags, or slight switchbacks. If you have a rolling slope, consider building a series of steps with one or more landings in the middle. For a long gradual bank, you may want to curve your steps to make them more interesting or alternate a set of small steps with a flagstone landing. If your slope is steep, build straight steps with "cheek walls" (small retaining walls) up the side to frame in the steps. Steps can also be built right into a retaining wall, providing access to higher areas.

I like to integrate the steps into the ground of the slope, stack stones in mortar for the riser, and use one or more smooth stones for the treads. Without a mortared riser, it's possible for the soil to wash out from under the treads over time, causing the treads to eventually shift and even become dangerously unsteady.

Since you won't have a concrete base from which to measure, you'll have to figure out the rise and run of your site to determine how many steps you'll need and the size of your treads and risers. Many gardening and landscaping books cover this topic in detail. In addition, *The Art & Craft of Stonework* by David Reed (Lark Books, 2002) provides thorough instructions for building dry-laid stone steps in a landscape. Use these instructions to dig a template for your steps into the soil before you begin so you can have a guide by which to set them. It's much easier to see the overall picture before the steps are set in stone, and you can make adjustments if you need to.

Think of the soil as the concrete block core. Starting at the top, set the riser first, then the tread stones on top of the riser. You'll need a mortar bed of 4 or 5 inches under the tread stones to make them solid. Work your way down the slope, setting risers and then tread stones. For these landscape steps, you probably won't have to veneer the sides (as you do for steps leading up to a building) unless the steps end up higher than the soil level in some places. If you can actually see the mortar bed under any portion of the stonework, veneer the side or add stone to cover up the mortar. Stone always looks better than a bed of mortar.

Metrics Conversion Chart

length

INCHES	MILLIMETERS (MM) CENTIMETERS (CM)	INCHES	MILLIMETERS (MM) CENTIMETERS (CM)	INCHES	MILLIMETERS (MM) CENTIMETERS (CM)
1/8	3 mm	7 1/2	19 cm	21	53.3
3/16	5 mm	8	20.3 cm	21 1/2	54.6
1/4	6 mm	8 1/2	21.6 cm	22	55 cm
5/16	8 mm	9	22.9 cm	22 1/2	57.2 cm
3/8	9.5 mm	9 1/2	24.1 cm	23	58.4 cm
7/16	1.1 cm	10	25.4 cm	23 1/2	59.7 cm
1/2	1.3 cm	10 1/2	26.7 cm	24	61 cm
9/16	1.4 cm	11	27.9 cm	24 1/2	62.2 cm
5/8	1.6 cm	11 1/2	29.2 cm	25	63.5 cm
11/16	1.7 cm	12	30.5 cm	25 1/2	64.8 cm
3/4	1.9 cm	12 1/2	31.8 cm	26	66 cm
13/16	2.1 cm	13	33 cm	26 1/2	67.3 cm
7/8	2.2 cm	13 1/2	34.3 cm	27	68.6 cm
15/16	2.4 cm	14	35.6 cm	27 1/2	69.9 cm
1	2.5 cm	14 1/2	36.8 cm	28	71.1 cm
1 1/2	3.8 cm	15	38.1 cm	28 1/2	72.4 cm
2	5 cm	15 1/2	39.4 cm	29	73.7 cm
2 1/2	6.4 cm	16	40.6 cm	29 1/2	74.9 cm
3	7.6 cm	16 1/2	41.9 cm	30	76.2 cm
3 1/2	8.9 cm	17	43.2 cm	30 1/2	77.5 cm
4	10.2 cm	17 1/2	44.5 cm	31	78.7 cm
4 1/2	11.4 cm	18	45.7 cm	31 1/2	80 cm
5	12.7 cm	18 1/2	47 cm	32	81.3 cm
5 1/2	14 cm	19	48.3 cm	32 1/2	82.6 cm
6	15.2 cm	19 1/2	49.5 cm	33	83.8 cm
6 1/2	16.5 cm	20	50.8 cm	33 1/2	85 cm
7	17.8 cm	20 1/2	52 cm	34	86.4 cm
				34 1/2	87.6 cm
				35	88.9 cm
				35 1/2	90.2 cm
				36	91.4 cm

length (formula)

U.S.	MULTIPLY BY	METRIC EQUIVALENT
Foot	0.3048	Meter
Yard	0.9144	Meter

area

U.S.	MULTIPLY BY	METRIC EQUIVALENT
Square inch	645.16	Square millimeter
Square foot	0.09290304	Square meter
Square yard	0.8361274	Square meter
Acre	0.40469	Hectare

mass

U.S.	MULTIPLY BY	METRIC EQUIVALENT
Ounce	0.02834952	Kilogram
Pound	0.45359237	Kilogram
Ton	0.9071847	Tonne

volume

U.S.	MULTIPLY BY	METRIC EQUIVALENT
Fluid ounce	29.57353	Milliliter
Gallon	3.785412	Liter
Cubic inch	16.387064	Cubic millimeter
Cubic foot	0.02831685	Cubic meter
Cubic yard	0.7645549	Cubic meter

temperature

FORMULA

Degrees Fahrenheit
Minus 32
Times 5
Divided by 9
Equals degrees celsius

Acknowledgments

I'd like to thank my father, **John Macfie**, and my uncle, **Jim Macfie**, for inspiring me in this craft. I would also like to thank my friends, contractors, and architects for giving me the opportunity to make a living at this.

A special thank you to **Cason Builders Supply of Hendersonville, NC**, for allowing us to photograph at their stone yard.

Thanks also to the following stone suppliers:

B&L Distributing Co. Inc
Brevard Lumber Company
J.R. Stone Sales Inc.
Jennings Building Supply
Norandex/Reynolds Distribution

Many thanks to the following homeowners who allowed us into their homes and yards to photograph their stonework:

Mr. and Mrs. J.W. Barnhill
Randy Baron, Brevard, NC
Peggy Bridges, Brevard, NC
Denise Byrd, Brevard, NC
Shepherd E. Colledge, Middleburg, FL
Art. G. Fisher, Asheville, NC
Neill and Miranda Fuleihan, Lake Toxaway, NC
Steve Hedden, Asheville, NC
Tee and Sherry Hooper, Greenville, SC
William R. Howell, Jacksonville, FL
James P. Macfie, Little River, NC
John A. Macfie, Penrose, NC
Kristi Pfeffer, Asheville, NC
Joanne and Robert Poston, Brevard, NC
Macon Construction, Inc., Penrose Quarry, Dahlonega, GA
D. Carroll Parker, Brevard, NC
Alfred F. Platt, Jr., Brevard, NC
Joanne and Robert Poston, Brevard, NC
Lance Ringhaver, Lake Toxaway, NC
Tim and Anna Robinson, Brevard, NC
Don and Mary Rose, Brevard, NC
Bonnie and Mike Vandegrift, Asheville, NC

Photo Credits

Thanks to the following photographers and stonemasons who contributed photographs:

Stewart O'Shields: 3, 49 (top), 53, 94, 95, 98, 105, 106, 114, 125 (left), 128 (top), 130, 136, 138, 154, 161, 168 (top)

Sean A. Trapp: 5, 6, 7, 9, 11, 12 (bottom), 13, 14, 15, 16, 17, 18, 19, 20, 21, 22, 23 (bottom left), 24, 25, 26, 27, 28, 29, 30, 31, 32, 33, 35, 36 , 37, 38, 39, 40, 42, 43, 44, 47 (left), 48 (lower left), 49 (bottom), 50, 52 (top left and bottom left), 54 (middle and bottom), 55, 56, 58, 59, 60 (top and bottom), 61, 62, 63, 64, 65, 67, 69, 74, 75, 76, 77, 78 (bottom), 79, 80, 81, 82, 83, 84, 86, 87, 88, 89, 90, 91, 92, 93, 96, 99, 100, 101, 102, 103, 104, 108, 109, 110, 111, 112, 115, 117, 118, 119, 120, 121, 122, 124 (top), 125 (top right, bottom right), 126, 128 (bottom left, bottom middle, bottom right), 129, 132, 133, 135, 139, 140, 142, 143, 144, 145, 146, 147, 150, 152, 154, 155, 156, 157, 158, 159, 160, 162, 163, 164, 165, 166, 167, 168 (bottom), 169, 170, 171, 172, 173

Alan Ash/Ash Stone Masonry: 51 (left)

Paul Bardagjy: 46, 148

Evan Bracken: 97

Bruce Brawley Masonry Inc.: 47 (right)

Bill Davis, Earth and Stone Masonry: 52 (bottom right)

Jamey DeMaria Masonry: 51 (right), 131, 151

Richard Gambino Stonemasonry: 10 (bottom), 54 (top)

Richard Hasselberg: 60 (middle), 68, 78 (top)

Dency Kane: 10 (top), 57 (bottom), 124 (bottom)

Paul T. McMahon: 12 (top)

Mark Smoljanovic/Kingsway Stone Masons Ltd.: 127

Roger Wade: 8 (photo by Roger Wade/Courtesy of Locati Architects and S.B. Construction), 48 (top) (photo by Roger Wade/Courtesy of Locati Architects and S.B. Construction), 113 (photo by Roger Wade/Courtesy of Carney Architects), 153 (photo by Roger Wade/Courtesy of Lachance Builders)

Thanks to **John Thelen of Landmark Landscapes of Swannanoa, NC**, for demonstrating how to excavate for a patio base.

Special thanks to my crew: Mitchell Macfie, Jason Altemose, Sam Benton, Dizaidel Berez, Rob Hellrigel, Flavio Lopez Luis, Leonardo Olmedo Luna, Benito Olmedo Luna, Miguel Olmedo Villarreal, Federico Olmedo Villarreal, Jose Rangel Bravo, Bernardo Olmedo Luna, Edgar Olmedo Luna, and Hugo Gallardo.

Index

693.1   Macfie, Cody,
MAC   1976-

Getting started with
mortared stonework.

$24.95

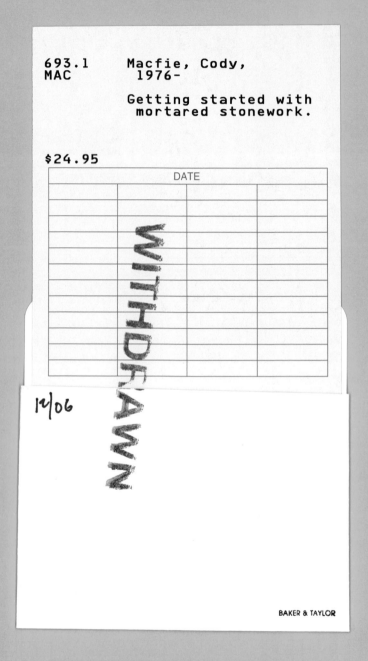

WITHDRAWN

12/06

BAKER & TAYLOR